Hope *for the*
Heavy Heart

Ellen Richardson

For the War-Weary and the Heaven-bent

TATE PUBLISHING & Enterprises

Hope for the Heavy Heart is just that, especially if you consider hope to be the firm expectation of future fulfillment rather than a mere wild fantasy that something good just might happen. Ellen offers both practical and spiritual insight that is rooted in her own generously offered history of deep struggle and heroic triumph. This is not a how-to manual, but a chronicle of and meditation on the nature of true healing.

-Greg Paul,
author of *God in the Alley*
(Shaw Books) and *The Twenty Piece Shuffle*(David C Cook).
Greg Paul is the founder of Sanctuary Ministries of Toronto, the current director of the organization and pastor of the Sanctuary community. Sanctuary makes a priority of welcoming and caring for some of the most hurting and excluded people in Toronto, including addicts, prostitutes, homeless men, women and youth, gay, lesbian, and transgendered people. In addition to maintaining and perpetuating the vision for Sanctuary, Greg's role includes pastoral care, counseling, leadership, organizational partnerships, fundraising, and representing Sanctuary to the public.

This book is a creative and very relevant look at a common human struggle—a struggle that requires divine intervention. Richardson describes an honest journey of challenges, defeats, and victories, yet captures glimpses of how God is at work in each phase. It's a must read for all who have walked the road of no return—a reminder that there is a way back.

-Dr. Jean Chamberlain Froese,
Executive Director—Save the Mothers (Uganda)
Assistant Professor, McMaster University
Dr. Jean Chamberlain Froese is the executive director of Save

the Mothers—an organization whose vision is that no mother or her child should die from preventable pregnancy complications. The program is committed to helping the neediest mothers of the world by leadership development, education and mobilization of influential professionals who can impact cultural and societal issues that contribute to the death of these vulnerable mothers. Please see www.savethemothers.org for more information.

On the Poetry Section

This poetry reads like medicine for your soul. Crafted from the journey of physical and emotional pain, Ellen's writing leads you to prayers of honesty and hope. She's living proof that we can do all things through Christ who strengthens us. Thank God for Ellen Richardson and her work.

-Lorna Dueck,
Listen Up TV

Published by Tate Publishing & Enterprises, LLC
127 E. Trade Center Terrace | Mustang, Oklahoma 73064 USA
1.888.361.9473 | www.tatepublishing.com

Tate Publishing is committed to excellence in the publishing industry. The company reflects the philosophy established by the founders, based on Psalm 68:11,
"The Lord gave the word and great was the company of those who published it."

Book design copyright © 2008 by Tate Publishing, LLC. All rights reserved.
Cover design by Nathan Harmony
Interior design by Jonathan Lindsey
Published in the United States of America

ISBN: 978-1-60604-911-2
1.Inspiration: Motivation: Autobiography
2. Christian Living: Spiritual Growth: Healing
08.11.10

This book is dedicated to all with heavy hearts, including those who have contemplated or tried to commit suicide, and their families. Also to those who have successfully completed the act and to their loved ones left behind.

Acknowledgments

I would like to thank my beloved ever-present friend and Savior, Jesus Christ, who truly works all things together for good. Secondly, I would like to thank my family for their love and support, especially in helping me achieve more independence. My mother and sister, in particular, helped me find and make a home, which has improved my quality of life so enormously, and for which I am eternally grateful. My brother and father have supported me both emotionally and financially, and I thank them so much for this. My father in particular has been a generous and steadfast support to me financially throughout my life.

I would like to thank the various wonderful people I have worked with over the years who have helped me become the person I am today: Sheila Ellis, chaplain at the Scarborough Hospital/Grace Division; Sandra Ricketts, my spiritual director of twelve years; Dr. Stephen Barsky, my psychiatrist for eleven years who supported me through my degrees; Keith Walker, my amazing psychologist from Lyndhurst Hospital; Orville Green, former Counseling Coordinator at Yonge Street Mission's Christian Community Centre; Paul Stevens, chaplain at the institution; Noemy Donan, my beloved social worker; Dr. Edward Kingstone, a psychiatrist who finally diagnosed the delusions after 11 months and who came to visit me at Lyndhurst on his off-time, and Dr. Sender Herschorn, who performed extensive bladder surgery on me and who has, as a result, improved my quality of life.

Friends who mean the world include Terry Patryluk, John Barnes, Lewis Boles, and Cheryl Flook, who have stood by me through thick and thin. Anne Eagles, a dear mentor, who tried to reach me while I was delusional, has been a great source of help. Beverley Pope is the world's greatest encourager and Randy Heinson is the world's kindest man. I thank Teerat Jackree, who worked with me at the institution and encouraged me to write, and I would also like to thank Karen Booth, who's love and support were especially precious. Special thanks as well, to Jill Goodman, my photographer.

Thanks also to Richard Tate and the Tate family for believing in me and my work.

Contents

Foreword

I will never forget coming back from being away only to learn of Ellen being in the hospital as a result of her suicide attempt—a jump from a downtown Toronto bridge. The fact that she was still alive was a miracle in itself. Ellen and I have crossed paths several times through the years, first having classes together at Bible college, and then when she was involved at our inner city mission church, and still today as friends.

Despite not having an easy life and thrown even more challenges, Ellen musters up the courage to take pen to paper and share her experience with mental illness and the issue of suicide. A topic not always favored by Christians, Ellen is brutally honest and tackles all the angles. It's obvious that God has journeyed with Ellen all the way, carrying her across valleys of despair and through the process of writing this book in which she weaves scriptures and spiritual guidance with her own thoughts and feelings so that she may comfort and help others.

Here, Ellen opens her heart with the hope to not only educate but share with you the sufferings of many of our communities. With Christ at the forefront, Ellen in her book shows that life, no matter how tough, can give glory to God.

Rev. Jan Rothenburger, Community Outreach Pastor Church @ the Mission, Yonge Street Mission, Toronto.

Jan works with those impoverished in all aspects, from those on the streets, to those in prison and everything in between.

Introduction

Psychiatrist Dr. M. Scott Peck begins his best-selling book *The Road Less Traveled* with three powerful words; "Life is difficult." This very truth lends itself to the idea that we can get fatigued, that we can experience a true weariness with life itself. We can get to the point, if we're honest with ourselves, where the very nature of pressing on becomes arduous, even agonizing, where we can tire and become exhausted with the relentless, ongoing race, where we can become war-weary and have thoughts of and longings for a heavenly home. The Bible describes heaven as a place of "no more death or mourning or crying or pain."[1] This can be a very attractive place indeed as we are foraging through this difficult and oftentimes messy life.

A line in the movie *The Princess Bride* says that life is pain, that anyone telling you anything different is trying to sell you something. Certainly, God said to Adam as a result of his sin in the Garden of Eden, "Cursed is the ground because of you; through *painful toil* you will eat of it all the days of your life"[2] (italics mine). To me, life is not only painful toil but joy and hope in Christ. However, given the facts that life, as we know it, is difficult and is pain, it's only natural that even the most stable and steady of minds can entertain thoughts and have wishes for a heavenly end. *Hope for the Heavy Heart* addresses those who find or have found themselves with burdens almost too much to bear. This book is geared for suffering souls who are seeking solace and companionship in their sorrows. It is for anyone who has ever contemplated or is currently considering suicide. Indeed it is for anyone who wants encouragement on his or her journey. I have, in fact, written this book also as encouragement to myself in my own walk. You see, I have experienced suicidal ideation countless times, having lived with a heavy heart most of my life, certainly as a child and then in later years.

My Story

We all encounter dysfunction in our families to one degree or another, since we are all born sinners. My parents could not teach what they did not know. They had experienced dysfunction in their own families of origin; coming from wounded backgrounds, and not having the opportunity to heal from them, they inadvertently passed on at least some of the wounding.

On top of their own wounds, and as well, being atheists and not having the love of God in their lives, they could hardly be expected to teach their children a strong spiritual foundation. My parents separated when I was four when, at which point I witnessed a serious altercation between my parents. They eventually divorced; it was and is not an amicable split.

My parents met my physical needs well; my father had a very strong work ethic, working as a professional engineer, having earned his Master's degree in Applied Science. My father was at one time a commanding officer in the Royal Canadian Air Force. He was very financially responsible, paying child support and alimony when he left the family home at the time of the marital separation. I saw my father on birthdays and holidays following a relatively brief period of time where he came for bi-weekly visits after work.

My mother prepared nutritious meals for us, with a fresh salad every dinner. She earned her Bachelor of Arts degree through night school after the separation, and her Bachelor of Fine Arts and Bachelor of Education with day classes. She worked as a supply teacher, mainly of Art and English, until she retired. My parents were, however, not so good at meeting my emotional and spiritual needs in my childhood.

My general experience of my parents in my childhood was that they were both generally angry, impatient, and unapproachable. I have known them only to have a strong hatred for each other. In addition, I experienced parentification, where I was thrust into a "caregiver" role for my struggling mother, something my Mom regrets doing today. My family also singled me out as a troubled child and gave me special attention, both positive and negative—positive as they supported me in my overt anxiety, negative in the form of scapegoating.

I went straight from high school into the Faculty of Nursing of University of Toronto in 1982. Living in a room off campus, I experienced a date rape shortly after the move. About a year later, the male therapist I had been working with asked me to describe in as great detail as possible how sexual relations would be between him and I.

Running from the therapist and into the arms of boy-friends, three monogamous relationships and two years later, I found myself pregnant after one night, despite having used contraception. I realized one night too late that this man, who would be the father of my only child, was merely using me. I decided after that night not to have anything to do with him. I gave birth without his support to a healthy baby girl on August 3, 1986, who I subsequently gave up for adoption.

I was officially diagnosed with major depression in my 20s. At age twenty-five, I made a serious suicide attempt in May 1989 while in hospital for depression, requiring fifty stitches to my wrists. About 1½ years later, I had a cult experience from November 1990 to February 1991, where I experienced auditory and visual hallucinations. I was pressured and agreed to go off my meds, not under-standing their importance for my mental health.

With the proper medication, I recovered and went on from September 1992–August 1998 to earn two degrees: a Bachelor of Religious Education with a Pastoral Focus and a Master of Divinity in Counseling, graduating with the title of individual, marriage, and family therapist. I continued to find healing through my own personal counseling and through spiritual direction, the latter of which I have been doing since 1996.

The rough draft of this book, including both the prose and the poetry, was written when I was living in an insti-tution from April 2002–December 2003, for what is now my second disability—paraplegia.

Perhaps you have seen the movie *A Beautiful Mind*. It is based on a true story of a brilliant mathematician named John Nash who suffered from a debilitating symptom of mental illness called delusions. Dr. Nash's illness was schizophrenia and mine is depression, yet delusions are common to both, as well as to manic depression or bipolar illness. Delusions signify acute psychosis.

I developed delusions in September of 2000. I spent eleven months in this state, during which I made an unprecedented bid to get help. I visited various emergency departments, making perhaps sixty specific and desperate pleas for psychiatric help, including calling 911 on myself a number of times. For the most part, I was sent home. Occasionally I was admitted to hospital, but there was to be no treatment for the delusions in that time span. Unbeknownst to me, I was part of a study that promoted in-community care of the mentally ill.

My relatives were at a loss to help me. My mother had, for example, flown to Europe for a six-week holiday when I was about eight months into the delusions. She was bewildered by my state but convinced that I was out of danger since I had told her after a near-fatal overdose at the six-month mark that I would "not do it again." My psychiatrist at the time refused me counseling though I had vehemently requested it. He also refused to refer me to another psychiatrist. He told me that "hospitalization is not an option" (taken from the hospital records, because I do not remember it), and took me off an antipsychotic medication, the very kind I required, stating that I did not need it.

During the second week of May 2001, on two separate occasions, I went to three different hospitals. I spoke openly of fears that I would again try to take my life, verbalizing a specific plan to jump off the Bloor Street Viaduct, a bridge which I will describe momentarily. On one occasion, I stated that if I was not hospitalized, I intended to jump from the Viaduct. Instead of being hospitalized, I was sent to a psychiatric crisis centre that was, in fact, walking distance from the very bridge I threatened to jump from. I left this centre and returned home only to, a few days later, call 911 on myself, again speaking openly of my desire to end my life with a jump from the bridge. Again, I was sent to the psychiatric crisis centre.

Following the second visit to the crisis centre that week, I walked from there to the bridge, and without hesitation, threw myself over. At that time, I believed I wasn't getting better because I was a failure to God, that I had, in fact, lost what I believed was God's fantastic future for me. A thought came into my mind as I approached the bridge, a thought which I now believe was planted by Satan, that if God did not want me to jump, he would provide someone on the bridge for me. There was no one, therefore, I concluded that it was God's will for me to jump. Paraplegia was the permanent result.

I remained psychotic for two months post-injury until I "fired" my psychiatrist and got a new one who diagnosed me properly and finally put me on the right antipsychotic medication.

This bridge, the Bloor Street Viaduct, in Toronto, Ontario, Canada was known for its lethality. It is estimated that one person had jumped from that bridge every twenty-two minutes. The Bloor Street Viaduct, or as it was known, Prince Edward Viaduct, was constructed in 1919 and was second only to the Golden Gate Bridge in San Francisco as a suicide magnet in North America. Around it now stands an extensive suicide barrier known as the "Luminous Veil," which was put in place at a cost of $6 million; it went up some two and a half years after my jump.

I speak at length of my trials to say, "I know heavy-heartedness." The LORD has been faithful and has brought me once again out of a pit: about two and a half years post-injury, I was referred to by a friend as "Ellen of Joy" (as opposed to "Helen of Troy"). About six years post-injury, I had helped over forty individuals come to faith in Christ; God has and is continuing to redeem and transform my life.

Some Scripture

Certainly, Jesus said, "In this world, you will have trouble. But take heart! I have overcome the world."[3] Or Ellen's paraphrase, "This life you lead is difficult. But take courage! Through clinging to Jesus, you too can find victory."

Jesus conquered Satan with the cross and the resurrection. By clinging to Jesus, He will lead us to victory, no matter what, though that victory may look unfamiliar or may take a form that is different than what we expect. Recall that forty people now know Christ because I am in a wheelchair.

Satan is a subtle and formidable, albeit defeated foe. Remember that Jesus had to come as a helpless baby and die the most excruciating death to counter the work prompted by the enemy in the Garden of Eden. It was, in fact, however, through the cross, through extreme suffering, that redemption was won, and as I've said, Satan was ultimately defeated. That is why we can find victory clinging to Jesus.

This is a book that points to the greatest burden-bearer of all time, Jesus Christ, and shouts that He is, "the way and the truth and the life,"[4] even in and through deep grief, pain, and sorrow. After all, He has said,

> *Come to me*, all you who are weary and burdened, and I will give you rest. Take my yoke upon you and learn from me, for I am gentle and humble in heart, and you will find rest for your souls. For my yoke is easy and my burden is light[5] (italics mine).

Scripture tells us, "(M)an is destined to die once, and after that to face judgment ..."[6] Death is a one-shot deal, and, I will argue, needs to be left in the hands of the Creator. "Through him (Jesus) all things were made; without him nothing was made that has been made."[7] Just as you did not "create" yourself and had no say in your creation, the time of and the way of your death needs to be left to Jesus. Paul said, "I eagerly expect and hope that I will in no way be ashamed, but will have sufficient courage so that now as always Christ will be exalted in my body, whether by life or by death."[8] Paul also said that your body is not your own, but is God's possession. "Do you not know that your body is a temple of the Holy Spirit, who is in you, whom you have received from God? You are not your own; you were bought at a price. Therefore honor God with your body."[9]

Jesus is not only Creator, He is Sustainer of all life: "Even to your old age and gray hairs I am he, I am he who will sustain you. I have made you and I will carry you; I will sustain you and I will rescue you."[10] Did you catch all the promises in this verse?

The Bible speaks of sharing in Christ's sufferings and of the coming glory: "Now if we are children, then we are heirs—heirs of God and co-heirs with Christ, if indeed we *share in his sufferings* in order that we may also *share in his glory*"[11] (italics mine). Indeed there will come a time, if we can hang on, when we will be ushered into "his glory."

The Apostle Paul cries out, "I want to know Christ and the power of his resurrection and the fellowship of *sharing in his sufferings*, becoming like him in his death, and so somehow to attain to the resurrection from the dead"[12] (italics mine). This has become my prayer as well.

I have slowly come to see that sharing in Christ's sufferings is a privilege. I truly believe that when I face Jesus on my Judgment Day, God will finally reveal to me His unfathomable, incomprehensible, eternal perspective. All will be made clear. I will, at that time, rejoice and thank Him for putting me through the trials He did. I pray for patience that I might hold on 'til that day.

You might ask, "How can I be assured that when I face my Judgment Day, that all will be made clear and I will rejoice?" or "But how can I hold on?" Answers to these questions and more you can find in the pages within. I invite you on a journey—with one who knows heavy-heartedness. Please note that Scripture is taken from the New International Version, the official version

of the Bible for the Bible College and Seminary when I
attended them.

Chapter 1: Patience

Remember that growth is measured over time. We talk about the growth of a child, for instance, not in terms of a daily change but over a period of time. Often, it's a span of many months or perhaps years that pass before we can say, "My, that child has really grown." So it is with adults on the spiritual level. Growth is a process and change is often slow and minute, difficult to measure. We may even need someone close to us to comment on the growth he or she has seen in us; it can be difficult for us to see it in ourselves.

God says, "Love is patient."[1] He lists "patient" first of all, for He knows how demanding we can be of Him, of others, and especially of ourselves. My roommate in the institution said, "God works slow but sure." God knows how impatient we are to get blessings, to get to where we want to go. He is, in fact, trying to mold in us patient endurance and give us a character of love in His eternal, unfathomable way. Author, artist, speaker and quadriplegic, Joni Eareckson Tada says that it is this character that is the only thing we will take with us when we die.

But we want answers, nay, demand answers from Him that we in our limited finite vision think we must have.

Keep in mind that God has an eternal perspective. What we want and feel we must have is not necessarily what He wants for us or gives us. We need to trust that He knows best in His eternality, something we will never grasp here on earth.

Be very careful: "Be very careful, then how you live— not as unwise but as wise, making the most of every opportunity, because the days are evil."[2] You and you alone are responsible for your actions. A suicide attempt has altered my life permanently and made it more challenging for God to bless me in the ways He wanted to. He created us and we will suffer, yes, but His desire is that we enjoy Him in His fullness, to really abound in the richness of His full blessings. Be patient in your pain, friend. Personally, when I am tempted to despair, I think of the blessings even in my suffering that, as I've said, after just over six years in the wheelchair, I have helped about forty people come to faith in Christ. Preacher John Hagee says, "When you're down to nothing, God is up to something." And yet we seek answers.

Sometimes, when things don't go as we had hoped, we can turn away from God or pummel Him with "why questions," not satisfied until we have *the* answer we are looking for. When others mistreat us, we can be quick to blame and curse. Or we can be quick to be understanding and forgiving and patient with others, even with God. But with ourselves—this is sometimes the most difficult hurdle. I recall that it took years for me to finally forgive myself for indirectly causing my own spinal cord injury.

Being kind to ourselves is especially difficult for those of us who have not been consistently treated with patience when we were growing up, but instead, encountered more criticism than loving responses. We can tend to sit in self-blame and emotional self-flagellation, actually reinforcing it because that is what is so familiar to us.

We can listen to the whispers of the enemy as he berates us; we can tend to do this as a form of emotional comfort food. Being put down is what we may be used to, so we take on this role for ourselves, listening to and embellishing on the negative "tapes" that play as a result of our early mistreatment. This tendency can go so deep and be so consuming. After years of therapy, I still find that Satan uses the "tapes" to trigger me at times at an unconscious level. Trust God to give you strength to fight the spiritual battle that Paul spoke of:

> "Finally, be strong in the LORD and in his mighty power. Put on the full armor of God so that you can take your stand against the devil's schemes. For our struggle is *not* against flesh and blood (people!), but against the rulers, against the authorities, against the powers of this dark world and against the spiritual forces of evil in the heavenly realms"[3] (amplification and italics mine).

I recall that when I told my story about the paralysis, most understood and accepted me readily, but I, for years after the injury, unconsciously hung on to self-condemnation. I would tend to give fuel to the "voices" that lingered from my past, that would diminish and demean me. Perhaps you find yourself doing something similar.

It took me a long time before I was able to feel enough

of God's love, to grow strong enough to recognize when I was doing this. I needed to be patient with myself as I learned not to feed into the lies of the enemy.

Dr. Charles Stanley, prolific author and pastor, says that God makes a promise. Faith believes it. Hope acknowledges it, and patience quietly waits for it. Cling to the promises of God, such as, "(H)e who began a good work in you will carry it on to completion until the day of Christ Jesus."[4] We all need to be patient with Him, with others, and with ourselves, and trust that He will bring us through. Someone said, "If God brings you to it, He will bring you through it."

Healthy Self-Love

Recall Jesus' teaching, which appears numerous times in Scripture, "Love your neighbor as *yourself*"[5] (italics mine). I believe God repeats Himself to emphasize the importance of this teaching. You are commanded not only to love your neighbor, but to love yourself too. If we have not had love consistently modeled for us in our childhoods, we are especially vulnerable as we fail to develop the inner "muscles" of healthy self-love.

As I've said, Satan can use the old negative "tapes," and self-love can be very foreign. Remember that God's Word tells us, "(T)here is now no condemnation for those who are in Christ Jesus."[6] The "voices" of condemnation do not come from God and do not fit us as children of God.

Healthy self-love involves accepting compliments and positive feedback from others, from God, and from yourself. It can feel very uncomfortable to sit with positives, especially if you have known more criticism than praise, particularly in your childhood. I found help to eventually accept the positives, to receive them, through counseling. I encountered a great capacity for healing in a healthy therapeutic relationship with a trained counselor. Personally, this has been essential to unpack, unravel, and express deep and complex emotions, particularly those associated with my family of origin.

Effective therapy can lessen the sting and diffuse the power and intensity of the negative "tapes," disarming the enemy who plants thoughts in our minds that enflame old hurts yet unexpressed. To me, it is these unexpressed, repressed emotions that create instability, added grief, and complication to my life. Healthy counseling provides a safe environment for me where hidden emotions become uncovered and can be finally expressed and released so that they do not inadvertently continue to run me. Being in counseling also helps me become a better therapist, as I learn what it is to sit in the "other seat." In fact, I continue in therapy simply because of the complexity involved in emotions, for deep support, and as well, because of the depth of the hurt I incurred as a child: "For lack of guidance a nation falls, but many advisers make victory sure."[7]

As I allow God to dig beneath the surface and into my unconscious, with the help of a good counselor, hurts can come up that need to be felt and experienced in order for me to find freedom. If these hurts remain in the unconscious unexpressed, they can inadvertently influence my behavior, as I've said, often in a negative way. For example, rage became unconsciously repressed because of the inadvertent, unintentional childhood mistreatment from my parents. When, for instance, I witnessed the altercation between my parents when I was four, the deep emotions of guilt, rage, and fear became repressed and were only uncovered with the help of counseling much later in my adult life when I was able to tolerate them. My unconscious repressed it because in my child-like mind, it felt unacceptable to be angry with the very people I needed so much, who I needed for my very survival. In counseling, I re-experienced these painful emotions as they came up to the surface to be healed, and so found that, in expressing them finally after years of repression, I was freed from them.

In addition, good counseling helped me to express my anger, for instance, in more healthy ways than the way my parents modeled for me. It seemed that the inappropriate ways of expressing certain emotions like anger had become engrained into my personality, and it was through good counseling that I was able to "unlearn" them and put new ones in their place.

For me, engaging in therapy is an embracing of the truths of human frailty, the need for help, and the complexity of emotions. It strikes me that seeking counseling is called "getting help" purely because that's what it is: it is getting help with our most difficult, powerful, and painful emotions.

Yet, I found that it takes time, patience, and practice to receive love and disregard negativity, especially because that's what I was used to listening to. As I've said, as a troubled child, I received special attention from my family, some positive, some negative. They offered me support in my overt anxiety, however, I was also thrust into the role of scapegoat in my family. It has been a life-long struggle to be able to accept godly love and receive goodness from Him. I have felt, in the past, that I was meant to be engulfed by negativity, that that was what I deserved. I developed "fear-heartedness" that was profound and far-reaching. Perhaps you can relate. If you are feeling especially vulnerable to attacks from Satan, know that you are not alone, that there is hope. Now I know that I am precious in God's sight and worthy of all of His best for me, that I am infinitely precious and eternally loved by the God of the universe, but to embrace this, as I've said, has been a lifelong struggle requiring patience. Patience is, in fact, a fruit of the Spirit (see Galatians 5:22–23) and is, I reiterate, the very definition of love as laid out in 1 Corinthians 13:4. To be patient with myself then, with yourself, is truly exercising healthy self-love.

Forgiveness

Very closely linked to having patience is the act and process of forgiveness. When someone hurts us, we, by a conscious act of our will, can forgive. However, there is also a process of forgiveness which involves working through the hurt feelings, anger perhaps, disappointment, etc., and choosing to let these feelings go, thereby embracing a new perspective in the relationship with this person who hurt us.

We can learn from the model of Jesus and His incredible capacity to forgive as an example. He said to those who put Him on the cross, "Father, forgive them for they do not know what they are doing."[8] This represents a conscious act of forgiveness. Recall also, however, the story of the Prodigal Son (see Luke 15:11–32). The son had taken his inheritance and squandered it. One can only imagine what the father had felt when his son demanded his share and walked away. Rather than reject him, upon the son's return, the father "was filled with compassion for him; he ran to his son, threw his arms around him and kissed him."[9] Though the Scripture doesn't say it here, likely there had taken place a process of forgiveness in the father, as he had worked through the feelings he had at seeing his son "take the money and run". Perhaps there was rage, at least disappointment, perhaps discouragement, but none of these feelings surfaced when the son returned, I suspect, as I've said, because there had been a working through that had taken place. I believe the father had undergone the process of forgiveness as he had had a change of heart that occurs with such a process in order to be able to embrace his son emotionally once again. The father in the story in the Prodigal Son is a model to us of forgiveness and its power.

If you have owned a particular sin in your life, addressed it by repenting of it, Jesus has forgiven you for it. "For as high as the heavens are above the earth, so great is his love for those who fear him; as far as the east is from the west, so far has he removed our transgressions from us."[10] Receive his forgiveness and let the shame wash away. This is a choice.

Perhaps you have negative "tapes" I spoke of in the previous section playing at full volume inside of you because you feel you have done something unimaginable and unforgivable. Perhaps you feel you have done something so terrible you cannot envision a forgiving Savior. He *is* a forgiving Savior. I've felt that in my own life. As I've said, I could not forgive myself for indirectly causing the spinal cord injury. Recall that Jesus says, "For if you forgive men when they sin against you, your heavenly Father will also forgive you. But if you do not forgive men their sins, your Father will not forgive your sins."[11] This is very strong language; I suspect He means also for me as well, and for yourself.

As I repented for my suicide attempt by an act of my will, I let the forgiveness I experienced in my spirit from Jesus be used as a model for my forgiving myself. As He encouraged me to receive His forgiveness, I let it wash over me, cleansing me, urging me to face my shame and remorse, as He led me to work these and other difficult feelings through in the process of forgiveness. This process, I should mention, can take days, weeks, months, or years, depending on the individual and the situation involved. It has taken years for me to not give power to the tendencies toward scapegoating myself, a pattern that I have profoundly engrained inside of me, not to go into self-blame but to receive His forgiveness on a deep level.

To not forgive yourself is to not receive the gift of forgiveness that Jesus has lovingly offered and further paid a high price to deliver. As I've said, certainly if we have not been treated consistently with love in our early years, to receive love in the form of forgiveness can be like venturing out into the unknown. We must have the same courage to embrace the new experiences that come from Christ as we did at the time of our conversion: "If anyone is in Christ, he is a new creation; the old has gone, the new has come."[12]

Corrie Ten Boom, author and survivor of the Holocaust, has said that when we confess our sins, God casts them into the deepest ocean, gone forever. And even though she says she cannot find a scripture for it, she believes God then places a sign out there that says, "No Fishing Allowed."

I'm amazed at how forgiveness is so paramount and an ongoing necessity, as layers upon layers of anger and pain are uncovered in me with respect to my childhood, begging me, each time, to come to Him. This is another reason why ongoing counseling has helped me so much. In addition, in this world full of trouble, the need for forgiveness within relationships comes up again and again.

Jesus urged, "Come to me, all you who are weary and burdened, and I will give you rest. Take my yoke upon you and learn from me, for I am gentle and humble in heart, and you will find rest for your souls. For my yoke is easy and my burden is light."[13] I find I come to Jesus when I work through difficult feelings in therapy and invite Him to heal and restore as I embrace the process of forgiveness.

Unforgivingness, whether it is for others, for God, or for self, is a heavy burden that inevitably causes weariness and indeed more problems for the one who has not forgiven, than for the offending party at whom the unforgivingness is directed. Allow Christ to embrace and take your pain, and watch, as He gives you lightness in your spirit in return. He alone can give you "a garment of praise instead of a spirit of despair."[14]

Just know that He can clear all the spiritual garbage from us: "If we confess our sins, he is faithful and just and will forgive us our sins, and purify us from all unrighteousness."[15] Notice that the Scripture says "all", not "some". Count on this; trust in this promise of God.

Mercy

In line with patience and forgiveness comes mercy. The Pharisees ask,

> "Why does your teacher eat with tax collectors and 'sinners'?" On hearing this, Jesus said, "It is not the healthy who need a doctor, but the sick. But go and learn what this means: 'I desire mercy, not sacrifice'. For I have not come to call the righteous but sinners."[16]

Just as Jesus bestows mercy on "sinners," so He is our example of how to treat others and ourselves:

> At one time we too were foolish, disobedient, deceived and enslaved by all kinds of passions and pleasures. We lived in malice and envy, being hated and hating one another. But when the kindness and love of God our Saviour appeared, he saved us, not because of righteous things we had done, but because of his mercy. [17]

We have to let down our pride and our tendency to run our lives by and for ourselves in order to receive from Jesus. In these verses, I also see that, as with patience, He is calling us to a merciful attitude toward ourselves, others, and Him. Recall the words of Jesus, "Blessed are the merciful, for they will be shown mercy,"[18] and "Be merciful, just as your Father is merciful."[19]

We can blame ourselves, others, and God, but He asks that we have faith, for it is the bridge between the temporal and the eternal. He accused his followers of "little faith"[20] and "rebuked them for their lack of faith."[21] Faith is exercised when one is merciful to self, to others and in one's approach to God.

In the temporal, we see with limited vision. Jesus has the full picture, an eternal perspective that, I emphasize, we will never have here on earth. I know you may be in relentless pain, but "I desire mercy not sacrifice"[22] could also relate to suicide, since suicide I see as the ultimate in self-sacrifice.

Mercy to me is forgiveness and love tied together inseparably. Suicide can be hatred, rage, anger, despair, sorrow, as examples, expressed in behavior. I have found that with help, with counseling, I have been able to dissipate the power of these difficult emotions so that I am less prone to act on them. The LORD created these emotions; He has a purpose in allowing us to feel them. I have experienced deep relief as I have faced these emotions in a safe and supportive environment. It strikes me that the psalmist, in expressing his pain, was able to find freedom and inevitably some resolution to his pain. I truly believe that it is precisely in the expression of the painful emotion that we can find release and freedom from its powerful grip on us. We can feel these emotions intensely, but we need not get stuck in them. He desires that you and I have mercy on others, on God, and, I believe, on ourselves, by educating ourselves about and embracing the emotions that terrorize us rather than make the ultimate sacrifice of self-destruction.

Recall, "(I)n wrath, remember mercy."[23] Habakkuk was praying to God at this time, but when I read this Scripture, God turned it around for me and suggested that I, in my anger, need to remember mercy—mercy to myself, to others, and to Him.

Jesus seeks your mercy to accomplish his good purposes. Had I not looked upon the professionals in the psychiatric system who had let me down with mercy and forgiveness, I would not have in turn felt mercy for those lost souls who God brought to me. As I've said, I was able to help introduce Jesus into the lives of over forty individuals about six years post-injury. Perhaps you have heard, "What goes around, comes around." He or she who has allowed themself to experience mercy is more apt to be able to show mercy. In addition, as I've quoted before, Jesus is merciful to those who show mercy. "Blessed are the merciful, for they will be shown mercy."[24] Certainly as well, in my case, God was merciful by sparing my life. I live and can reach out to help others, where I could easily have died or have been more seriously hurt, as with a brain injury.

He accomplishes his purposes as we surrender such powerful emotions as anger and rage at the offending party to Him and seek His mercy. And He promises that his purposes are good: "'For I know the plans I have for you,' declares the LORD, 'plans to prosper you and not to harm you, plans to give you hope and a future.'"[25] It's important to cling to the promises of God to give us strength in our spirit to handle the deep emotions that pain us so.

Being merciful to yourself includes embracing the very facts that you are good, ("God saw all that he had made, and it was very good"[26]), and that He is good, ("I am the good shepherd"[27]), no matter what the trial. Doubt may tempt, especially in periods of deep grief, but let this come and go. It is not from God.

Though He may allow suffering, deep suffering, and wrenching emotions, He is prospering you and wishing to make you rich in Him as you share in His pain.

"(R)ejoice that you participate in the sufferings of Christ, so that you may be overjoyed when his glory is revealed."[28] Perhaps you feel that to "rejoice" is a tall order at this time. Just know that when your time comes to leave this earth, "when his glory is revealed," you, as a Christian, will rejoice and be glad you endured. May we learn to face, to surrender painful emotions, and be merciful with ourselves, with others, and with the incomprehensible, uniquely eternal Him.

Chapter 2: On Accepting– Part 1

I repeat Dr. M. Scott Peck's words: "Life is difficult." This fact can be seen all around us: in tsunamis, earthquakes, hurricanes, personal tragedies, and serious health problems, as examples. Suffering is everywhere; recall Jesus words in John 16:33, promising that "in this world you will have trouble." I recall, in her book, *On Death and Dying*, Elizabeth Kubler-Ross states the five stages of grief: denial, anger, bargaining, depression, and acceptance. Accepting your losses is the final step as you work through difficult emotions such as anger and depression and come more to grips with your reality.

Can we embrace and accept that "life is difficult" as an objective fact? Can we objectify "life" and see it clearly for what it is? Recall that Jesus said, "(T)he truth will set you free."[1] That life is difficult is a truth.

I said to one client that he was scapegoated in his family not because he deserved it but because life is difficult and people make choices. We can make a choice to stop blaming, and in turn, do the spiritual work, especially when things don't go our way. I reiterate, "For our struggle is not against flesh and blood, but against the rulers, against the authorities, against the powers of this dark world and against the spiritual forces of evil in the heavenly realms."[2] Trying to understand and accept yourself through the lens of faith, through eyes the Spirit gives us, is so key.

God does require of us a great deal just to keep ourselves on an even keel. Recall, as a result of Adam's disobedience in the Garden of Eden, God said, "Cursed is the ground because of you; through painful toil you will eat of it all the days of your life."[3] Certainly if we plow a field and leave it, weeds grow. Silver tarnishes if buffed and left to sit. Rust seems to just happen on our cars, and mold appears if food is kept even in the fridge for some time. Recall the saying, "A rolling stone gathers no moss."

The world is often throwing "spiritual dirt" at me; it is my responsibility to regularly and routinely give it to God and let Him cleanse. This is why He offers the Bible, the Holy Spirit who can reside within us to guide, comfort, and strengthen, and this is why he provides other people, particularly the Body of Christ, with whom we can fellowship and worship.

Jesus suggests that we take it in day chunks: "(D)o not worry about tomorrow, for tomorrow will worry about itself. Each day has enough trouble of its own."[4] Perhaps when very heavy-hearted, we need to break it down into an hour-by-hour, even minute-by-minute journey—this unique and completely individual journey that you are on.

Only One You

Imagine, in all eternity, there is and will ever be only one you! You are an original who has a set of circumstances and reactions that are absolutely and entirely unique to you! You have a personality including strengths, weaknesses, likes and dislikes that is entirely yours and yours alone. In fact, hurts in your life are also yours and are your responsibility, no matter how they got there! You cannot choose how you have your start, but you can choose what you are going to do with the cards you've been dealt.

You have experienced circumstances with a unique set of reactions all your own, for which you are ultimately responsible. What an awesome task! What enormous loneliness! God gives us the Holy Spirit to actually live within us, to be in our breath, to come alongside us so we do not collapse from loneliness. And He has promised to "never leave (us) ... nor forsake (us)."[5]

As with you, I did not have perfect parents—mistakes were made, difficult emotions became repressed within me, and my spirit was muddied. It is for these reasons that I personally sought out counseling for myself, as I've mentioned, especially since I had not been, in my childhood, consistently modeled healthy love or an understanding of the spiritual nature of conflict, as laid out in Ephesians 6:12, quoted above.

When I was an unbeliever, I merely talked about my feelings in therapy, not within a spiritual context. I seek individual counseling now with a godly, praying therapist: I say godly because I prefer someone who is taking his or her leading from the Holy Spirit, and praying, because God can use prayer in such profound ways to promote and invite healing. Since we are in a spiritual war, these two characteristics in a therapist, to me, are now indispensable.

A godly, therapeutic environment can offer me the deep acceptance, warmth, and safety of Christ, in which I can explore and embrace previously hidden, deep pain. Therapy can be long-term, but it can also simply last for a short period of several weeks in times of a crisis. Entering into it requires a certain degree of humility and courage as one comes to a recognition that he or she has come to the end of themself and the need for a "two-person approach" to a particular problem. I remain in counseling today because I can encounter deep problems that trigger previously hidden layers of dysfunction that come up to be healed.

I have found that it is imperative for me to choose a counselor who has a clear understanding of the spiritual nature of conflict, as laid out in Ephesians 6:12, both interpersonal, between two people in a relationship, and intrapersonal, within the soul of one individual, i.e. the war within against Satan where we need to rely on the Holy Spirit. As a result of this, it is imperative for me that I seek help from a counselor who relies on the Holy Spirit for guidance. Having God as the third person in the counseling session is a must in my books.

To further clarify, especially when I am in pain due to a crisis or other deep trouble in my life, difficult emotions from the past that lie hidden can be triggered and can come out in ways that may be surprising in their power. A journey through the "valley of the shadow of death"[6] can further bring up pain yet unresolved. This can make life that much more difficult and complicated, adding to the fact that life, in itself, is already difficult. Painful emotions can block up the works like a clog in my spiritual drainpipe. Deep pain from my past fueled my desire for health and wholeness; I did not have many in my life who offered me the emotional safety and consistency I found in counseling. Many can find healing in relationships outside the therapeutic forum, especially when healthy relationships are modeled in the family of origin; this was not the case for me. I chose to face myself with the help of counseling.

For me, finding expression for hurt emotions long repressed was the beginning of deep healing that led to a more satisfying, productive, and peace-filled life. It worked to give me strength and self-control, to prevent me from having fits of rage, which are listed as one of the "acts of the sinful nature,"[7] and a root of bitterness, both of which do not fit me as a child of God. Scripture says, "Get rid of all bitterness, rage and anger, brawling and slander, along with every form of malice."[8] Again, the Word of God reads, "See to it that no one misses the grace of God and that no bitter root grows up to cause trouble and defile many."[9] I needed help to be able to become aware of and alter my unhealthy patterns of handling my emotions, to develop more healthily. Perhaps you feel a nudging in your spirit; I offer you my experience with counseling as an option only to that end. Remember, there is only one you. You are on a wholly unique and individual journey. We were made to work interdependently with one another. Again, I have found the therapeutic relationship, when it's healthy, to be an incredible, sometimes surprising, enormously comforting source of healing.

Spiritual Warfare

The mind is the battlefield where Satan targets and plants his seeds to trigger and try to dominate the emotions. It is as we feed the Spirit of God in us, as Christians, through a daily regimen of Bible reading, prayer, perhaps godly music, reading, and fellowship that we find strength to cope with the attacks of Satan in our minds and to face the emotions that threaten to debilitate us.

Beware—it bears repeating that Satan is a subtle and formidable foe, albeit a defeated one. Remember that Jesus had to come as a vulnerable baby and die the most horrible and agonizing death willingly to counteract the work of Satan in the Garden of Eden with Adam and Eve. We can embrace that life is difficult by educating ourselves through reading, studying, and meditating on the Bible as well as seeking His will in a dialogue of prayer that involves petition, thanksgiving, and listening to His voice. It is truly in clinging to Jesus that we find victory since He, once and for all, defeated Satan through the cross and subsequent resurrection.

In speaking to God in prayer, through Jesus, we can find peace:

> Do not be anxious about anything, but in everything, by prayer and petition, with thanksgiving, present your requests to God. And the peace of God, which transcends all understanding, will guard your hearts and your minds in Christ Jesus. [10]

When I read this while I was in the institution, it dawned

on me that this is a formula. As I sought Him diligently, He did, in fact, grant me His peace. Fervent prayer is so important; it can help us use wisdom and care in our relationships where the spiritual battle is often at its most intense.

Because life is difficult and spiritual warfare is a reality, thoughts of suicide and the act itself I see as really just a part of this life. Intense pain can drive us to the very end of ourselves. Your enemy and mine would use that state to torment and belittle to the point where we can feel convinced that ending our life is the best solution.

As I've said, Satan uses the mind to influence the emotions: he seeks to disappoint then discourage, then he tries to keep a person in despair long enough that it leads to a desire to die, which he hopes would end in the person's death by his or her own hand. I understand if you are or have felt this way. I'm here to say that there is another solution than death, but the truth is, it means engaging in spiritual warfare, where attitude is so key, which we will discuss in the following chapter.

Chapter 3: On Accepting– Part 2

I have found that accepting at my core that life is difficult was so crucial. Let me explain what I mean by this. By this, I mean developing appropriate attitudes. I used to believe that because I had suffered in my life, I had a right to expect that things should go my way. I was wrong. As long as I am on this earth, I will encounter difficulty. I reiterate Jesus' words: "In this world you will have trouble."[1] The key is attitude; what I do with what comes my way.

An Attitude of Gratitude

Years ago God led me to develop an attitude of gratitude. I live my life by the verse, "Give thanks in all circumstances."[2] I even have a carving of that verse on the wall in my living room.

I heard a story of Satan taking someone on a tour of his lair. There they saw a room full of his "seeds." The person asked Satan what this was, to which Satan responded,

"Those are the seeds that could not be planted because of grateful hearts."

This attitude of gratitude helped pull me out of a deep depression when I was newly injured with the spinal cord injury. I was able to give thanks for a functional wheelchair to get around in, that I was not quadriplegic, that I was not bedridden.

Can you find things for which to give God thanks, even something small and seemingly insignificant? There is a song that says, "Count your blessings, name them one by one, and it will surprise you what the LORD hath done." Indeed, I have found that as I start doing this, I, in turn, find more and more for which to give God thanks.

And there are blessings that you probably do not consider, such as the ability for your body to change position when you sleep, for example. Being able-bodied, you can turn your body at night automatically—something you perhaps have never considered a blessing. I have to turn myself manually and use strategically-placed pillows to prevent pressure sores. "Count your blessings, name them one by one, and it will surprise you what the LORD hath done." Surely in doing this, you may be amazed as to just how many there are.

An Attitude of Prayer

The verse directly preceding, "Give thanks in all circumstances" is "pray continually."[3] I believe this refers to an attitude of prayer, that we are to keep our gaze on the LORD and have Him in the forefront of our minds, being willing to pray about anything and everything at anytime.

I did not have many people to talk to when I was growing up. In my teens, I trusted people too easily and too quickly because I was so needy. When I met Jesus, I was so thrilled to have an inner person to whom I could go and who could be with me wherever I went, whatever I did, whatever I thought and felt.

Today I go to Him regularly, for bigger decisions and even for smaller ones. It is so comforting to know that I can go to Him day or night—about anything—and He will respond in loving-kindness, attentiveness, and patience, which was lacking in consistency in my earlier years.

With this attitude of prayer, I can sense His comforting ever-presence that helps me manage and face painful realities, such as my aloneness. He can comfort and soothe me in my aloneness like no other. Truly, with Jesus, I am never actually alone. No one person can be there for us like He can. And prayer develops and increases intimacy with the one who knows all. Despite the fact that He knows all, it is His desire for us to commune with Him, in sharing our hearts, and in listening to His still, small voice in a beautiful dialogue as we develop an attitude of prayer.

Suffering as a Calling

Another attitude that can help us when trials come our way is to embrace them as a calling from God to share in His sufferings. God says, "(I)f you suffer for doing good and you endure it, this is commendable before God. To this you were called, because Christ suffered for you, leaving you an example, that you should follow in his steps."[4]

Do we spend time complaining about our trials, and taking little action, or do we immediately see the hand of God in situations He brings us to? When we see our sufferings as a calling, this attitude can help us dig our feet in, and stand in the midst of it, as outlined in Scripture. "Therefore put on the full armor of God, so that when the day of evil comes, you may be able to stand your ground, and after you have done everything, to stand."[5] If something happened to you that was beyond your control, know that God is wanting to use it to call you to a deeper walk with Him; He is indeed calling you to Himself.

Putting Parents into Perspective

I mentioned earlier that we need to accept that life is difficult "at the core;" by this, I feel that we need to accept our parents with their failings and weaknesses. This attitude led me to sort through my feelings for my parents. It meant letting go of blame and taking responsibility for any hurt or distress within me, regardless of how it got there.

I needed to acknowledge that my parents tried their best, and I let go of child-like expectations for perfection. I took my eyes off my parents and placed them on the only perfect one, Jesus Christ. To face at my core that life is difficult is to embrace my parents and any pain that I incurred as a child, to work it through and to learn from it, so I do not repeat any abuse or habitual wrong-doing. I use the present tense here because, as I've said, I'm amazed that there are layers of dysfunction that come up even today and beg to be healed on new levels.

Because I did not have many others consistently and deeply supporting me in my past, I tended to confront difficult and powerful feelings in a healthy, therapeutic environment. Now I have friends who support me, including a spiritual mother. But the therapeutic environment offers me a place to do the most major and deepest work as trust is built in safety without the insecurity of measuring up in a friendship. Spiritual direction, which I will speak more on later, also has provided me with an avenue for deep healing.

I have found that working through childhood pain is excruciating, but I have come to see that I have to relive it to come through it. I suffered a kind of death, a loss of innocence, when my vulnerability as a child was mishandled. I need to work through the difficult emotions that resulted and became repressed in order to find life and freedom again in my spirit.

One who holds on to rage and resentment for past wounds and does not embrace the decision and process of forgiveness, as I've said, ultimately hurts themself the most, though this person also spreads an ill wind or "fragrance" around himself/herself.

The process of forgiveness encompassed, for me, a working through of waves of anger and bitterness to come to a peaceful shore. I truly believe that God calls us to this so that we can get to know Him more intimately here, and so, relate to Him better when we are called home. (I refer you here to the poem *Eternal Love*.) Only when I could see past the mistakes of my parents, feel the rage, talk, release it, and find forgiveness in my spirit—only then was I truly set free. For me, it was in a healthy therapeutic setting that I found this release. I don't mean to keep harping on it, but therapy has been indispensable and so essential for me. It has been a tool for me of a sometimes surprising power and healing capacity. For you, it may be with a trusted friend or other relative, though I honestly feel that deeper healing can take place in therapy simply because of the safety and consistency I can find in it.

Jesus says, "(T)he truth will set you free."[6] Accepting my truth means going deeper than the intellectual; it means embracing through the spirit the emotions that are there, including hurts that are buried. I reached out for help to embrace the suffering that I incurred as a child as something going on in me that affects the way I interact with others.

I was raised in a home where my parents were ignorant of God and His Ways. Satan encompassed them in their own pain. Both my parents were ill-equipped, to raise spiritually healthy children. I believe that "truth" again speaks to the fact that all people have been given free-will to accept or reject the help and love Christ offers. They have chosen not to receive Him. This is to me a sad and tragic reality that is my "truth," which I must embrace to truly find freedom.

In terms of emotional health, however, my parents were unable to process their own childhood hurts perhaps partly, if not totally, because it was frowned upon in their generation to seek emotional help. If it became known that you were seeing a psychiatrist, you could be ostracized from people. Today, it is much more widely accepted to receive help to find resolution to deep, underlying hurts. I was able to work through and process repressed hurts that resulted from unintentional mistakes. I was then well on my way to accepting "at my core" that life is difficult.

Personal benefits of seeking counseling have been numerous. It has helped me to grow as I have gained confidence and faced fears that hindered me. It has helped me, in turn, deal responsibly with self-control and not reactively to difficult and pressure-filled situations. And counseling has helped me see myself as separate from my parents, from my family. Growing up as I did, enmeshed or too close, parentified and scapegoated, I had to develop healthy boundaries somehow. Accepting my separateness from my parents and my family, I was forced to look at my loneliness as well. Not connecting healthily with my parents in my childhood, my loneliness was an open wound. In addition, on occasion I would sense jealousy from my Mom—jealousy of the attention potential friends paid to me, so I did not have many of them growing up.

Godly counseling brought God into my loneliness and into my pain. I was able, for instance, to envision Jesus' healing presence in the room when I witnessed the altercation between my parents. Certainly, godly counseling allowed the presence of another person, a safe, compassionate, Christ-centered person to come into my hurts as well. All this has eased the pain of loneliness, as the counselor brought his/her and Christ's presence into my world. As I shared, this person would absorb some of my pain, and I would feel God's compassion toward me with my wounds. I recall one therapist I know who had on his wall a plaque that said, "A trouble shared is a trouble halved." With a godly, praying therapist, I experienced God's grace and love in the midst of my suffering.

I still have vulnerabilities and can be triggered, but I have developed a deeper understanding and felt intense healing. In addition, God has granted me more of all of the fruits of the Spirit[7], especially self-control, patience, joy, and peace, as I have put my parents into perspective with the help, especially of godly counseling.

Chapter 4: On Accepting– Part 3

For Parents

I have not raised children. Given that, I have a limited perspective. However, I have come to the understanding that just as it is an awesome, sometimes lonely responsibility to care well for oneself, it is doubly so for parents who are responsible for other lives. In light of this, I offer a few words of encouragement, especially to parents.

If parents truly accept at their core that life is hard, as I've just described, they can spare the children from feeling the harshness of difficult adult life, freeing them to run and romp as children should.

Seeking to resolve deep issues in a responsible way, parents can function as a buffer, protecting their children from the harsh reality that is life. This is especially important for parents, because you likely do not want to pass on unresolved hurt to the next generation. As a parent, committed to the process of healing, you then can act as a cushion between your child and reality.

Abuse is committed for a number of reasons. Unresolved hurt can trigger unhealthy responses, perhaps because the person has an unconscious expectation or attitude that life ought to be something different than it is, that life ought to go his or her way or be kinder to him or her. When there is a total acceptance that life is difficult and responsibility taken for his or her hurts, there is a freedom that comes for the children of such parents as these. It is actually unresolved hurt, as I've said, that can result in inappropriate behavior patterns being carried over to the children.

My mother was scapegoated as a child and unwittingly passed this on to the next generation. She did not have the chance to resolve her childhood wounds before she set to raising her children. I was forever changed because of this. My deep-seated fear and lack of connection with people as a result of the scapegoating I received manifested itself in me for years, in that I developed dependent relationships, had low self-esteem, and was unable to assert myself. This consequently led to my being used and abused by people with predatory tendencies.

The greatest thing that a parent can pass on to their children, aside from a knowledge and an experience of Jesus, is the ability to be assertive. I experienced so much unnecessary pain in my life—the date rape, the abuse from my first therapist, and the pregnancy, as examples—all were associated with the fact that I was unable to assert myself, and I was therefore taken advantage of.

If parents do not embrace their emotional and spiritual responsibilities to their children, their child's world can be openly exposed to harsh realities that can plunge the child into sadness, anxiety, even depression. In time, as the child becomes an adult, he or she may feel ill-equipped to handle life's storms when they come, not feeling the security necessary to be prepared for the fact that life is difficult at a deep level, since that was not modeled.

The adult may unconsciously believe that life should go his or her way and be kind because he or she had it so hard. If there is even a shred of this belief in a person, he or she can experience life not as difficult as should be expected, but as generally tortuous and unmanageable. This I believe can contribute to a suicidal predisposition I will speak about later.

To reiterate then, because my parents did not have the chance to work through their childhood hurts that resulted from the dysfunction in their own families of origin and lacked the spiritual understanding of Ephesians 6:12, they were not prepared for the rigors of rearing emotionally and spiritually healthy children. I developed the very notion that I had it tough enough, that life should be kind to me because of it. This attitude I picked up from my parents through the unconscious, as they had not, in my opinion, embraced that life is difficult at what I've called their "cores."

I did not have in my unconscious—I had not objectified—at a deep level that life is very difficult, so when I found it so, I reacted to things going really bad as if they were intolerable and unlivable. I developed the belief and held it in the back of my mind that if things got severely difficult, I could always commit suicide. And I tried, as I've said, on three separate occasions. It took a suicide attempt that altered my life radically to alter that deep-seated belief.

Parents, in particular, need to take seriously their responsibility to themselves first of all, because they are being watched very carefully. They are being modeled. A suicide attempt from a parent can send the message to the children that when life is tough, it's okay to give up, and can lead a greater likelihood or temptation for that child when he/she is grown to think of and indeed commit suicide.

Parents need also, of course, to be responsible to their children both emotionally and spiritually, so their children can be protected, directed, and prepared for adulthood in a world where life is indeed difficult. I do tend to think, though, that leading by example is the most powerful way to teach and in turn take responsibility for your children. I would encourage you, if you are a parent, to allow your children to know about the struggles you face, not to lean on them for support, but in order that they may see you, and God in action. As the children witness your dependence on God and interdependence with each other in a world where real problems exist, they can learn appropriate coping skills as they grow.

Prior to my paralysis, I had not embraced at my core that things getting severely difficult is just a normal part of life that I ought to expect. I do firmly believe that this attitude contributed, if not resulted in my suicide attempts. Parents especially need to accept the difficulty of life since they can be particularly vulnerable to despair because of the relentless needs presented by their children. But with God's strength, drawing from the courage Jesus showed at Gethsemane (Matthew 26:36–46, for example), and on the cross (Matthew 27:32–54, for example), we can endure. As I've said, I do not have children I have raised, but I am responsible for my paralysis, something that can tempt me to despair at times. Remember that what you do has effects on those around you, not just parents to children, but adult to adult. The damage that is caused for the child, though, by a parent's suicide attempt, is so profound. As I've said, growing up, the child can develop an attitude that when the going gets tough, it's okay to bail out. This is not the message you want to relay to anyone, let alone your children, I'm sure. And what a strong and wonderful heritage you leave your children if you endure to the very end, until God takes you home in His time, in His way.

On Parentification

In my view, it is never appropriate for you to look directly to your young children for support. As well, young children do not need "friends" in parents, they need "parenting" parents. They need firm but kind discipline, not to be seen as an "equal" who can give adult support. Support can come inadvertently as the sensitive, caring child interacts with his or her parent. I'm not referring to this but rather to a leaning on your young child by subjecting him or her to serious, heavy, adult problems and expecting the child to respond as a support. As I've said, sharing your struggles with your child, I believe, is actually good so they can see God in action, but to expect your child to get involved, and not merely witness and watch, is a mistake.

This promotes parentification, where the child strains to care for his or her caregiver purely for self-preservation. A child can feel tortured when unconsciously he or she puts in all sorts of energy into helping and uplifting the parent, because his or her very survival depends on that parent. Parentification robs a child of the innocence and carefree nature of a healthy childhood. My mother, out of her loneliness and desperation, told me of her adult problems starting when I was very young, perhaps five or six. She has since admitted that this was a failing of hers and regrets doing it.

You may feel abandoned spiritually and emotionally. You may feel alone as perhaps my mother did when she was raising me or as I experienced as a child. You may have a hard time coping in that aloneness. May I caution you again not to lean on your young children. They need to witness a solid dependence on God and a healthy interdependence between adults in order to mature healthily; they do not need to strain under the weight of adult problems with which their immature, fragile spirits are ill-equipped to cope. Just as we as adults cannot tolerate knowing the mind of God and the eternal reasons for what He does, so the young child's mind needs to be protected from burdens that are beyond his or her capacity to healthily embrace.

On Feelings

Maybe you have been physically abandoned, or perhaps you were emotionally and spiritually left at a young age. My father left the home when I was four, and my mother, facing the task of parenting alone to a large degree, was unable to be emotionally and spiritually present for her children. My Mom was and is without Jesus, as well. As a Christian, remember that with God you are never alone.[1] Even though you do not feel the Spirit, He is with you. He is there, regardless of what your feelings may be telling you.

In fact, as you struggle with deep feelings, feed the spirit through such things as prayer, fasting, Bible reading, and fellowship. As you do this, you will notice God supplying strength for you to face those difficult feelings. With Paul, I offer this: "I pray that out of his glorious riches he may strengthen you with power through his Spirit in your inner being, so that Christ may dwell in your hearts through faith."[2]

I have said that if I have learned anything from the jump, it is not to act on my feelings. Feelings come and go, they ebb and flow. Only Jesus is unchangeable, "the same yesterday and today and forever."[3] He is the rock on which we are to stand. He is our refuge. He is our fortress. I use the first person plural here, "our," because it is in community that we triumph. Through interdependent interaction with the members and leaders in my church as I've trusted God for His direction, He has in turn granted me such strength and stability that have helped make up for the lack of these things earlier in my family of origin.

Just after I became paralyzed, I was encouraged to rejoin my church by a woman named Beverley Pope, who I have said in the "Acknowledgments" section is the world's greatest encourager. She gently assured me that my church comprised my spiritual family, and that I ought to return. God used many to support; I found God raising me out of those feelings of depression and isolation caused by the paralysis, to come to a point where I was referred to eventually as "Ellen of Joy."

Perhaps you are feeling that your life is intolerable and unlivable. Counter those feelings with, to reiterate, the attitude that life in itself is difficult. There are days, for everyone, when we must take it hour by hour, even minute by minute, when it is relentless agony to go on. You are not alone in your pain.

I know that feeling, and I encourage you to cling to Christ and to Scripture. He is the resource. He is the great burden-bearer. He will take your pain as you surrender it into His capable hands and raise you up as He did me. He is the one who performs miracles in our hearts. He is the one who gives us the strength, the courage when we ask for it. He uses His Word to encourage, to speak individually to us in our pain. He tailor-makes the way He delivers His compassion to suit the unique originals that you and I are.

Paul writes, "And we know that in all things God works for the good of those who love him, who have been called according to his purpose."⁴ If we really sit with this verse and allow it to seep into our very pores, there is no need to remain in regret, especially if we also believe that God's control of our lives is sovereign. We may make mistakes and initially feel some regret, but we don't need to stay there, because we serve such an amazing God who can turn our most profound mistakes and failures to be our greatest victories, as He has done with me.

You, however, may be wondering where the good is in your situation. Truth is, you may not even taste of the "good" in terms of feelings while you are on this earth in the physical realm, especially if you are expecting ease, comfort, and pleasure. Certainly I do not feel "comfortable" sitting in this chair, and my life I would not describe as filled with ease. But in the eternal realm, I trust that God is forging good in my soul through my battered spirit and body, indeed through my suffering. You are more than your feelings; trust God, not them. Recall Proverbs 3:5–6: "Trust in the LORD with all your heart and lean not on your own understanding; in all your ways acknowledge him, and he will make your paths straight." Set your heart toward trusting Him, not indulging your feelings.

Chapter 5: Suicide Prevention

Are you now or have you ever wished your life would end? Are you thinking or have you thought about bringing your life to a premature close? When I felt like this after my spinal cord injury, a "friend" said to me, "Why don't you just commit suicide? You've been thinking about it for so long, why don't you just go ahead and do it?"

At that moment, though suicidal, I found myself speechless, hesitating. In hindsight, I could see that my unconscious, at that time, was drawn toward thinking up reasons why I shouldn't commit suicide. It got me in touch with the part of me that I did not think existed at the time, the part that still wants to live.

It was a shock to me in my suicidal state to hear encouragement for my thoughts, but this ignited something within me, some will to live, however tiny. I was surprised to see this in myself at the time.

Perhaps you too feel like life is not worth living. Perhaps you too can sense something stirring deeply within you as you imagine someone saying to you the words my "friend" spoke.

On Inching Forward

When we are or have felt suicidal, inching forward can be the best we can do, especially in the face of bombarding questions. How many times have I wondered how I could have done things differently? How much have I tormented myself, flagellating myself, feeding into the negativity and denigration that ultimately comes from the enemy but felt natural because of the criticism I received as a youngster? I have a "ridiculing machine" in my mind that I'm prone to listen to since that was the type of thing I encountered sometimes as a child, particularly as a scapegoat.

It almost feels like a comfort to self-flagellate on an emotional level; it's what I was used to, it's where I felt at home. Does this really fit who I am as a child of God, as a blood-bought, infinitely precious child of the living God? If you can relate to this "ridiculing machine" and you are a child of God, does it fit who you are? Does it please God?

With all this negativity, I had moments when I tried to figure out if life was worthy of going on. I tried to decipher if I was worthy of going on. Fundamentally, I felt so unloved and unlovable, ugly really inside and out, that I really wondered if I was worth the fuss. Sometimes I didn't feel like I was worth the effort to go on. I didn't feel like I was worth the trouble when things got really tough. I always believed that suicide was a viable option if things got too difficult, perhaps in part at least because at the core, I did not believe that I was worth the trouble.

Looking back, with such events as the separation and eventual divorce eroding them, my parents responded understandably but reactively often with impatience and anger when I was a child. I found I eventually carried this over to God. Unconsciously, in approaching God, I felt afraid that I would get a similar response, feeling unworthy of being given time and effort.

Sometimes, as a child, I was a nuisance on purpose because this was a way I could get attention, albeit negative attention. I guess I felt as though negative attention was better than none. I had a tendency to want to be a problem to side with the negative messages I was getting and feel okay, to feel supported in a twisted sense. I could not feel that I was "good," so I sometimes would resign myself to my "badness." This is how I was at times, when I look back.

I outgrew this behavior, thankfully, but today, I can still catch myself feeding into the negativity, condemning, chastising, or belittling myself. I can feed into the lies of the enemy that were planted deeply, ultimately by him so many years ago. It is at these times that moving forward is very difficult, when I must go inch by inch, watching diligently for the "mines" that Satan tries to lay. Perhaps you can relate.

Now, I resign myself to just taking one day at a time—inch by God-given inch some days. As Charles Stanley says, life isn't about "ease, comfort, and pleasure." It's about crawling forward, sometimes painfully scraping your elbows and knees. It's about inching forward, seeking God to direct you just on to the next step.

Surrender–Part 1

An important step in the healing process is that of surrender. I reiterate Dr. M. Scott Peck's exclamation that life is difficult. Sometimes going on seems like relentless agony, virtually an impossibility. Sometimes we feel that things are not going to get better. Those who suffer with such ailments as paralysis, MS, ALS, or Cerebral Palsy, as examples, bear a heavy load. Jesus has spoken about healing. In fact, many have been healed, including paralytics like me.[1] As I surrender the reality of my paralysis to Jesus, I must also let the reality of miracles sit with me and give me support and hope.

Scripture does say that Jesus healed "many,"[2] not all. It is possible that God may choose to keep you in your present physical condition; He may improve and heal, and He may allow the status quo, even deterioration.

Remember, and I point out again, Scripture does not say "in some things," but "*in all things*, God works for the good of those who love him, who have been called according to his purpose"[3] (italics mine). Simply know that, whatever the situation, He will use it for His glory, no matter what, as you give it all to Him. Love Him by surrendering all to Him. To love Him is to let Him help you.

God may not choose to eradicate your physical suffering, for instance, but He will use it for His purposes, and He will change your attitude regarding your suffering as you surrender fully and let God have it. Holding back in anger, resentment, and bitterness toward God can prevent Him from flowing freely in your life. It can block the

Holy Spirit from transforming, renewing, and building you up.

Early on in my paralysis, I doubted the very existence of a loving Heavenly Father who could have allowed such devastation, such ruin to come to my life. I even cursed Him, said I did not love Him, and that I would never forgive Him for allowing me to go into this chair. Bitterness came knocking on my door. It was through Christian counseling, which involved surrendering that unforgivingness, that bitterness to God, that I was able to work this pain through and come to see that the feelings I was experiencing were normal given the circumstances.

I was also tormented for some time after the injury by regular thoughts of suicide. Over time, with counseling again, God helped me to see, as I surrendered my paralysis to Him, that it just better equipped me to serve others. It gave me a "deeper voice," that the wheelchair was a vehicle to access the hearts of a sect of society that I would previously not have known how to address.

God let me know that I could not have related to and subsequently reached out to comfort those in profound suffering had I not encountered it myself. My suffering merely makes me better equipped to be used of God as an instrument of truth and a more credible comforter to those in deep and relentless agony:

> Praise be to the God and Father of our LORD Jesus Christ, the Father of compassion and the God of all comfort, who comforts us in all our troubles, so that we can comfort those in any trouble with the comfort we ourselves have received from God. For just as the sufferings of

Christ flow over into our lives, so also through
Christ our comfort overflows. [4]

As I laid down my burden, His comfort trickled, then
poured in and through me to others.

My struggle involves laying down self-will and self-
direction and surrendering all my suffering into the
hands of a loving God. This surrender, in turn, allows
me to access more fully His omnipotent nature: "for the
battle is the LORD's"[5] and "(f)or the battle is not yours
but God's."[6] Letting Him carry me is a privilege of being
a child of God.

I'm reminded here of the prose called, Footprints by
Margaret Fishback Powers:

> One night a man had a dream. He dreamed
> he was walking along a beach with the LORD.
> Across the sky flashed scenes from his life. For
> each scene, he noticed two sets of footprints
> in the sand: one belonging to him and the
> other to the LORD. When the last scene of his
> life flashed before him, he looked back at the
> footprints in the sand. He noticed that many
> times along the path of his life, there was only
> one set of footprints. He also noticed that it
> happened at the lowest and saddest times in his
> life. This really bothered him and he questioned
> the LORD about it. "LORD, you said that once
> I decided to follow you, you'd walk with me all
> the way. But I have noticed that during the most
> troublesome times of my life, there is only one
> set of footprints. I don't understand why when I
> need you most you would leave me."

The LORD replied, "My son, my precious child, I love you and I would never leave you. During your times of trial and suffering, when you see only one set of footprints, it was then that I carried you."

Let Him and His strength carry you as you lay down your burdens at the foot of the cross. Someone wise once told me to do just that and not pick them up again. How often do we lay them down only to retrieve them up again in frustration at God's timing or His seeming "incompetence" or inability to "solve" our problem in the way we think it should be done? Remember, God's ways and thoughts are not our own. They are unique to Him, the eternal Creator. Let Him be God in your life. Let Him be the mystery that He is. Just trust in faith, something sometimes very difficult to do.

Friend, your body may remain in its broken state and that choice that brought so much pain cannot be undone, but God will heal the inner brokenness, your spirit, as you surrender your suffering to Him, all of it. It may take years to do this, to adjust to your injury or the condition in which you find yourself. In the following section, I would like to, first, introduce you to first a friend of mine, and then we will look into the Scripture to further illustrate this point.

Surrender–Part 2

Karen Booth

I had a friend named Karen Booth who lived in the same institution from which I came. She had had a stroke three days after she had open-heart surgery when she was thirty-eight. She became unable to use her hands, her vocal cords, her legs, and she was virtually blind. Her mind, though, remained keen and bright.

Attached to her wheelchair, she had a paper with the alphabet sectioned into three. To communicate with her, you needed to ask her which section the first letter of the first word that she wanted to communicate came from. She would let you know whether it was from section one, two, or three with a nod or a shake of her head. You needed to do this with each letter of each word she wanted to "say."

She could mouth certain letters, so certain people very close to her could communicate with her faster. She had completely accepted her lot in life and had completely surrendered it to Jesus. She was a strong believer. She forged ahead one day at a time, while still living in the institution, robbed of privacy and foundational quiet on a daily basis. She lived there for twenty-two years. She had a single room, but doors remained open for staff monitoring of patients. On a constant basis she had to listen to noises from the halls, at nights as well. Despite all this, she most often greeted me with smiles and laughter when I would visit. She died just as I was making the final edit on this book. She was and remains a testament to the resilience of the human spirit and to the power of God's Spirit living within an individual. She was and remains an inspiration to me as God used her brokenness and her courage to inspire others. He can do the same with yours.

Paul

Remember, three times Paul asked for his "thorn in the flesh"[7] to be taken from him. Jesus simply replied, "My grace is sufficient for you, for my power is made perfect in weakness."[8] Again, God may not take your suffering away, but He will give you the grace to endure it, if you will trust Him with it.

Paul goes on:

> Therefore I will boast all the more gladly about my weaknesses, so that Christ's power may rest on me. That is why, for Christ's sake, I delight in weaknesses, in insults, in hardships, in persecution, in difficulties. For when I am weak, then I am strong.[9]

We must bear in mind that this comes from a man who had suffered so much. For a list of his hardships, see 2 Corinthians 11:16:33. He was even in prison, where he wrote, "I have learned the secret of being content in any and every situation, whether well fed or hungry, whether living in plenty or in want. I can do everything through him who gives me strength."[10] Scripture doesn't speak directly of Paul's surrendering his suffering to Christ, but from this verse, I believe it is highly likely. By surrendering our suffering to Christ, we too can find great strength.

Paul actually boasts about his sufferings, including the equally seemingly outrageous, "If I must boast, I will boast of the things that show my weakness."[11] This goes against everything the world values in a man—power, strength, virility. In embracing his weakness, Paul was actually given these qualities and could exclaim, "For when I am weak, then I am strong."[12] There can indeed be great power in someone who embraces his or her weakness.

I have gained more of Him in my inner woman in such a way that could only be accomplished through the surrender of my suffering and an embracing of my weakness as Paul did of his. I have gained fruits of the Spirit (see Galatians 5:22–23), such as a deep and abiding joy of the LORD that truly is my strength.[13] Certainly, I am "being transformed into his likeness with ever-increasing glory ..."[14] I reiterate what Joni Eareckson Tada has said, that we will only take with us when we die bits of His character, so truly it is this that is of the very most value.

I have learned about the plight of the "homeless," those in institutions. I have learned about the pain of the mentally ill on a much deeper level. God has brought me through these situations as I gave it all to Him, surrendering self for Him and His guidance and strength. Don't doubt that he can do the same for you.

Chapter 6: I am Richer

I am richer now and for all eternity because of my suffering. I share with you now a passage that has become so dear to my heart.

> But whatever was to my profit, I now consider loss for the sake of Christ. What is more, I consider everything a loss compared to the surpassing greatness of knowing Christ, Jesus my LORD, for whose sake I have lost all things.

> I consider them rubbish, that I may gain Christ and be found in him, not having a righteousness of my own that comes from the law, but that which is through faith in Christ—the righteousness that comes from God and is by faith.

> I want to know Christ and the power of his resurrection and the fellowship of sharing in his sufferings, becoming like him in his death, and so, somehow, to attain to the resurrection from the dead.[1]

Everything that does not help me know Christ, I believe with Paul, is like refuse to me. That I may gain Him in my character is of eternal value that I cannot yet fully grasp here on this earth, yet I will one day know. Experiencing and sharing in His sufferings gets me closer to Him. It helps me to relate to Him better now and when I get to eternity. (I refer you here to the poem *Eternal Love*.)

I believe I have shared in His sufferings, having been exposed to that which breaks the heart of God, such as "homeless," displaced people living in very difficult institutional settings as I've mentioned earlier, and the neglect and abuse of the vulnerable and disabled, both psychiatrically and physically.

I am richer in my understanding of God's pain and am richer in my ability to relate to Him and His creation—people, people in pain. Again, He can do it for you. He can make you an instrument of comfort for those who suffer in similar ways to you. Hang on and let God be God, let Him work in you and in the situation. You'll be richer for it now, and then, when your Judgment Day comes! Realize that you will be spending a lot more time with Him on the other side of eternity than you will here. As Rick Warren says, and as I speak of later, this life is but a preparation for the next. I have a friend who says, "One day, we will laugh!" He's much bigger than you, He's much bigger than your problems—believe that!

Spiritual Transformation

Jesus can take your big problem and do a miracle of spiritual transformation. I believe that great suffering is an opportunity to draw near to God and watch Him work His transforming power in our lives. God healed each depression I encountered prior to the wheelchair enough to allow me to complete two degrees, seeking my support mainly from professionals. Some have said this accomplishment was a miracle.

During the first couple of months into my paralysis, I was still psychotic, planning still on this fantastic future, which included marrying my friend named Rob, becoming millionaires, having two children, a farm, horses, a sailboat, and dancing ballet! When I was finally given the appropriate medication, my delusions lifted, and I was faced with the reality that not only was I not going to have this fantastic future, but I was permanently disabled and could not go back to live in my home.

I was in a great and grievous depression, regularly having thoughts of suicide, finding my life so distasteful. Even sleep was not an escape as it had previously been because now, physically disabled, I was awakened several times a night to be turned to prevent bedsores and to be catheterized. Living independently seemed an impossibility; I believed that I would be institutionalized for the rest of my life. But slowly, as I worked in counseling, as I journalized and continued with spiritual direction, God raised me up.

Two and a half years after the injury, I moved from a long-term care facility to a one-bedroom apartment with attendant-care available to me 24 hours a day. It was a bit shaky at first, but now I do my own cooking, laundry, and shopping. Another year later, as I've mentioned, a friend referred to me as "Ellen of Joy."

It was at that time, about three and a half years post-injury, I even came to a point where I felt my spirit rise out of the wheelchair and stand. This occurred as I was watching the movie, *The Passion of the Christ*. The following day, I received prayer for healing of my paralysis. Later that same day, I felt my spirit get up out of bed and walk around in my apartment. My body then reminded me that I was paralyzed. Now I can "walk" and "run" and "fly" because of the transformation the Spirit has wrought inside of me.

Certainly, in my dreams as I lay sleeping, I am walking. I often have a sense, though in the dream that it is unusual for me to be walking. I honestly think that as I've come more and more to master the care of my paralysis and surrender my pain to Him through godly counseling, that I, in essence, "earn my legs" by learning to live without the use of them (I cannot bear weight at all). God redeems me and makes it okay that I am disabled in body. Four and a half years post-injury, I came to a peace about my condition as I could see the hand of God clearly working through it in my life in my family, with my friends. (Notice the progression over time in learning to accept and embrace my disability, emphasizing again that "God works slow but sure" and of my need for patience.) Complications from my paralysis such as the ongoing risk of bed sores, bladder problems, and mobility issues still have the potential to get me down at times, but I don't stay down. Usually these periods of discouragement and even despair come and go relatively quickly. God has given me a buoyancy and resilience in my spirit that only He could give.

Though I may be physically paralyzed, I am not spiritually, and it is in my spirit that God causes me to soar.

We cannot fly in our bodies. In that sense, even the able-bodied are limited. But with Jesus, we surely can in our spirits. He did it for me time and again. Believe that He can do this spiritual transformation for you too. Pray that He will do a miracle in your heart.

I Was Wrong; Now I Know

Simply because of Jesus' transforming power in the lives of those who follow Him, in my life, and of His ability to change my attitude about my suffering, I know now that I was wrong to try to end my life. In the movie, *A Beautiful Mind*, John Nash came to an understanding of his illness. I truly believe that that understanding was right around the corner for me and Satan knew it, so he tempted me to the ultimate in self-destruction.

I had a friend who believed that if she committed suicide, she would go to hell. But I had studied the Scripture: I believed that no one could snatch me from His hand[2] and that I could not escape from the love of God.[3] There was no one verse or commandment saying, "You shall not kill yourself." There is the Sixth Commandment: "You shall not murder."[4] It has been said that suicide is murder of self. Yet, I did not believe suicide was a sin. I believed that I would go directly into the arms of Jesus when I tried to take my life, without hesitation from Jesus or my need for repentance.

I had a liberal view of suicide. It was this liberal theology which almost killed me.

Charles Stanley says that liberal theology is an attack on the Word of God. I believed that God would completely understand in compassion and receive me into His kingdom. Perhaps He would have, had I died, but the point is that I presumed upon my salvation. I took advantage of the fact that I had been born again, sealed for all eternity, and that therefore, dying by my own hand was okay, that I would still see heaven. God is the one who decides who will and when, we go to heaven. Though I believe in eternal security, that once saved always saved, it is nothing to take advantage of and bank on because we want an exit from our pain. I understand the longing for heaven, but I believe now that suicide is a sin and therefore hated in the sight of God.

I realized that suicide is a sin when I needed forgiveness from God for the suicide attempt. In a service at church some months after I was injured, I felt I had to repent, almost to accept Jesus into my heart all over again, because the spiritual damage was just that profound. I found that after I did that, my spirit cried with sorrow for having jumped and with gratitude at my life having been spared. I was forgiven and I received it.

> (S)ince we have a great high priest who has gone through the heavens, Jesus the Son of God, let us hold firmly to the faith we profess. For we do not have a high priest who is unable to sympathize with our weaknesses, but we have one who has been tempted in every way, just as we are—yet was without sin.[5]

Jesus knows pain; He knows your pain. You can, therefore, trust him with it. We can glean strength from the endurance of Jesus, "May the LORD direct ... (our) hearts

into God's love and Christ's perseverance."[6] I pray this
for both you and I.

I never would have imagined previously that I would
have needed forgiveness from God for a suicide attempt
before I did it. With my two previous attempts, it did
not strike me that I needed to repent. When I became
paralyzed, my grief was just that much more profound,
and I felt God urge to come to Him with my remorse.
Fundamentally, I see now that suicide hurts my relationship to Jesus. When we hurt ourselves, we hurt His
creation (see John 1:3), His creation which is He called
"good,"[7] His creation which is "fearfully and wonderfully
made."[8]

Paul tells us: "Do you not know that your body is the
temple of the Holy Spirit, who is in you, whom you have
received from God? *You are not your own*; you were bought
at a price. Therefore honor God with your body"[9] (italics
mine). Remember, you are God's possession. I reiterate:
just as we did not "create" ourselves and "will ourselves"
into being, so the way we leave this world should be left
in the hands of the Creator. "Your" life is not your own
to take. I would go so far as to say that the most intimate
and personal parts of you are also intricately connected to
your loved ones and friends.

People who care about you have made a personal
investment into you, sharing with you, communing with
you, hanging out with you. You would not only dishonor
God if you harmed yourself, but those who have invested
in you, your parents or guardians as well, those who cared
for you when you were entirely helpless.

Remember the Fifth Commandment, "Honor
your father and your mother."[10] Suicide is not honor-

ing them. In their senior years, they may in turn need
you. I am grieved that now that my parents are getting
on, there is only so much I can do for them, being disabled. Think twice about what you would do to those left
behind, including your parents if you exited this world
prematurely.

If you feel helpless today to the point of wanting to
end your life, know that you are not alone. I have felt
these feelings. Many others have as well. In addition,
indeed, whether disabled or not, we are all helpless before
Almighty God. There is a song that says, "You (God)
alone keep the world from crumbling into dust." Certainly
we have witnessed this firsthand with the high number of
natural disasters, such as tsunamis, earthquakes, and hurricanes that the world has encountered in the first few
years of the second millennium.

Charles Stanley says that nothing happens that is
outside of God's permissive will. Know that you are in
His hand, that He is indeed in control. Your feelings of
hopelessness are not a surprise to Him, but they are just
that—feelings that change with the tide of emotion that
rises and recedes within us. Give them to Him. Let Him
take them and carry you. Then watch as He performs as
He does, miracles in your heart, as I've said, that only He
can do. Don't make a mistake like the one I made. I was
wrong: now I know, after the fact. Suicide is the enemy's
work. Instead, reach out to Jesus who cares for you in an
eternal kind of way—a way so big and so high that you
cannot possibly even fully grasp.

Know as well that everyone's life is not ideal. No one
has the ideal life. Everyone suffers. You are not alone.

Chapter 7: I Fought Suicide

In the years prior to the injury, I had preached about suicide as "the permanent solution to a temporary problem." I had twice read and did a book report on Joni Eareckson Tada's book, *When is it Right to Die?* I agreed with her stance against such things as suicide and euthanasia. Though I did not consider suicide a sin at that time, I had not been willing to date a man who had made several attempts because I felt that I was, in a roundabout way, condoning the behavior.

I had studied the Bible about prophets who became suicidal and recognized God's urging to take rest and food. I believed suicide was murder of self and therefore against the Ten Commandments. I fought suicide when I was in my right mind.

The Definition of Insanity

The media portrays the insane as someone running and screaming or babbling confusedly to themselves. I think insanity is not necessarily that dramatic. The Concise Oxford Dictionary says that "insane" refers to "not of sound mind, mad."[1] Allow me to describe the delusional world I lived in, and the circumstances that resulted from it.

I believed that the "Kingdom of Heaven on Earth" came down to heal me in a specific way. I would also call it "The Way of the LORD." I believed that I was somehow "chosen," that God had deemed me "special" because He revealed this amazing world to me.

The voices would use the name Rob, so I came to believe that someone named Rob was going to come into my life and that I would be married to him. I remember questioning this for a time, but I convinced myself that the Holy Spirit told me it was real. I believed the Holy Spirit directed me to some prints I had in my home, one called, Everlasting by a Robert Bishop, the others by a George Raab. As well, the first syllable in the tongues I spoke was Rob. I believed that the Holy Spirit used these facts to reveal to me that it made sense that the name of my God-chosen husband would be Rob. I felt also that the Holy Spirit unfolded that we were going to have two children, a farm, a sailboat, horses, and be millionaires. Who wouldn't want to believe in a world like that?

I came to feel that in order for the two of us to meet, I had to choose enough Rob things: certain foods and drinks represented Rob, like chicken and coffee, and certain TV programs were Rob, such as the news. There was contrarily an evil presence called "man." The voices would say, "Watch out for man." I again came to believe that "man" represented flesh and lust, evil desires opposite of that which I was to have for the partner God had chosen for me.

I believed that God would supply all my needs. I received this promise while I was in the hospital in September, 2000. The Holy Spirit had revealed to me as well, I thought, that I would receive a Bible from the community. I had previously gone around the hospital looking for one. On one of my passes from the hospital, I went to visit an Iranian couple who had befriended me. They gave me back the Bible I had previously given them. This I felt was God's Bible to me. The delusions further deepened.

Colors meant certain things. If I would see red in the public, I would think that that meant that I was in sin at that moment. Yellow meant cowardice and blue meant depression.

All the while, I had been going to various emergency departments of different hospitals to try to get treatment. I would often be sent home untreated. On occasion, I would be hospitalized, but still there was no clinician, up to that point, who picked up on my delusional state.

At the six-month mark, after losing the psychiatric day program which I had been attending for a couple of months, I tried to take my life, this time with a large bottle of antidepressants. I also took sedatives, so I slept for seven hours with the medication inside of me.

When I awoke, I immediately tried to suffocate myself. I couldn't kill myself this way, so I screamed. I could not stand or get out of bed, so I rolled myself out of bed. I couldn't use the rotary phone in my bedroom because my hand was shaking so much, so I crawled to the dining room and used the touch-tone one there to dial 911.

I was told by a nurse in the hospital that it was a miracle that I survived because I had taken so much and that it was in my system overnight. It was because the pills failed to do the job that I decided to jump from a bridge known for its lethality. I spoke openly to the professionals after the overdose about hearing voices but still did not receive proper treatment.

Eight months into the delusions, a Christian friend of mine that I had known for thirteen odd years came back into my life and wanted to date me. His name was—you guessed it—Rob! I assumed immediately that he was "the" Rob or whom the "Way of the LORD" had been preparing me for. I was ecstatic and dated him. Shortly thereafter, I went to his house and said outright that he was not taking our relationship seriously enough, that I had been "in training for eight months to be his wife," and that there were two lives depending on us, that we were going to have two children. Despite his bewilderment, we continued to pursue a relationship.

I was hospitalized actually three months before the jump, where, in one of my last ditch efforts to help myself, I wrote down the delusional world I lived in, including my ill belief that all black people represented the devil, and gave it to the doctor for him to decide if it was sickness or not. That particular doctor prescribed Haldol for me, a drug that would have pulled me out of the delusions. However, I was soon discharged into the care of my psychiatrist who promptly took me off the Haldol, saying that I didn't need it. Up to this point, I had been toying with the idea that my problem was medication-related. When my psychiatrist, whom I trusted, said that I did not need an antipsychotic medication, the delusions deepened even further, with me assuming all the more that I wasn't getting better because I was making foolish choices.

The jump was precipitated because the voices said that I had lost Rob because of the choices I had made. I believed it was the Holy Spirit that had told me this. I felt that as surely as I had "earned" him, I had lost him. I often felt as if I should be somewhere else aside from where I was, and that I wasn't getting well and experiencing the healing that God had promised because I was failing God. For instance, when I was with Rob one night, I heard the voices say that we were supposed to be at the symphony that night. I assumed the reason we were not was because I had somehow failed. This type of thing was a regular occurrence in my delusional world, contributing to my belief that I was a failure.

My family, meanwhile, did not know how to cope with my insanity. They made specific attempts to interact with me during the delusional period, but in the end, did not know what to do. In addition, it was coming up on Mother's Day, a time of pain for me as a birthmother. I knew I would suffer pain on that day and I felt I could not take it as well as the progressive feeling of failure that I had.

All these things caused me to be "insane," in my opinion. The decision I made to take my own life was based on feelings, delusional ideas, and stress-related pressures, not in the truth that God loved me, had called me, had a plan for my life,[2] and was there in the midst of it.[3] Scripture clearly says, "(J)oin with me in suffering for the gospel, by the power of God, who has saved us and called us to a holy life—not because of anything we have done but because of his own purpose and grace."[4]

A verse alluded to above goes like this: "'For I know the plans I have for you,' declares the LORD, 'plans to prosper you and not to harm you, plans to give you hope and a future.'"[5] I believe that the definition of prosperity here may not necessarily mean worldly wealth but rather spiritual riches that He hones in your character through suffering that calls you to Him. During the delusional period, I could not escape the torment of the voices long enough to receive such truths.

It was my dear mother who actually supported me in "firing" the psychiatrist I had when I jumped. God gave me a new one who, so thankfully, diagnosed the delusions finally, after eleven months and prescribed the proper medication. It was in enduring the ongoing trial of the paralysis and of life in the institution that God gave me inspiration to write the rough draft of this book of prose and of poetry. And it was in persevering that God grew me up so that my faith embraced new dimensions of pain all around me, to see and have a heart for anguish in whatever form it took, and to subsequently reach out with Jesus' love. To emphasize again, He can do miracles in your heart too, if you let Him, if you'll trust Him in and through your trial.

My decisions to end my life with pills and on the bridge were made when I was "insane," when my mind was not within my control. Those decisions were inevitably based on lies, confusion, and despair, as the enemy used my illness. I need to, however, now embrace the consequences, the reality of my paralysis, and let God use it for His purposes, to fulfill the promise of Jeremiah

29:11 of "hope and a future" that still stands and applies to me even now in my life. Perhaps you or your loved one has been or is "insane." Be very careful. A person who is not in control of his or her mind can do drastic and "crazy" things. This person needs to be protected and, via an advocate, led to receive the proper help.

Chapter 8: In the Case of Mental Illness

The unrelenting nature of the pain of mental illness coupled with the inactivity of professionals can certainly lead to drastic acts. In order to be and stay informed about their mental illness, patients need to engage with a competent professional as was modeled in the movie, *A Beautiful Mind.* John Nash had the support and understanding of his psychiatrist. This is so crucial as the mentally ill person is like a child—little red riding hood lost in the woods with a wolf chasing her. The ill person, though, needs to be able to articulate if and when he or she has suicidal ideation. Certainly part of the responsibility rests on him or her.

Often what is needed is a corporate hand of love to be extended. The ill one needs those around him or her to be actively loving, not passively watching and waiting, hoping the person deals with the illness himself or herself. Family and friends need to step in and insist that the person get the care he or she needs. Do not shy away from a more active advocate-type role. It could mean life or death for your loved one.

There can be a tendency to hurry the patient through the emergency department visit, placate, and send the patient "off to bed with milk and cookies." I was not taken seriously when I was crying out for help, even verbalizing my desire to jump. Consequently I did, and it is me and my family and friends who will suffer the cost for the rest of my life. Practitioners, take your role seriously. A person in acute psychological sickness requires your strong and supportive hand to lead him or her through the "maze of mental illness" and back to health.

What to Say

Family members noticing some unusual behavior from their ill relative ought to be on the alert and make concerted attempts to protect their relative. It is often heard that people say, "I didn't know what to say" when confronted with a person with acute mental illness. People divulged later that they felt that way about me when they encountered me in a psychotic state.

If I may suggest: speak from your heart. Tell the ill one that you feel tongue-tied. Reiterate your love and concern. Say it directly with words. Don't assume that the ill person should just "know" your feelings towards him or her. You can say how you feel seeing the ill one in his or her condition. Certainly I found that many wrote me off when I was psychiatrically ill. Enter in, take heart, and be a friend to the wounded one. He or she is not so different from you. Perhaps, as it was in my case, with the ill one, the root cause of the problem may be as simple as a biochemical imbalance.

With the mentally ill, even professionals sometimes don't ask the proper questions. Professionals, if there is some confusion about a client's state of mind, ask something like, "Describe the world you live in." There is a stream of counseling that suggests that you go along with an ill person's delusional ideas. It is so important that the ill one realizes that it is a result of mental illness that his or her thinking is skewed. To go along with these ideas is to enable, to encourage the illness. You need to pay attention to what you are hearing, and if what you are hearing is beyond your scope of expertise to diagnose, get another appropriate professional involved. Do it for the life of your client.

There was a professional I would go to for counseling when I was psychotic. I had been working with her for many years. She knew me when I was well. At no time did she suggest to me that my strange thoughts might be a result of mental illness. Instead, she would often go along with me. I believe there was a time when she confronted me on my saying that I believed I would marry a "Rob" for instance, but at no time, to my knowledge, did she suggest I might be delusional or get a second opinion to help her clarify and assess my state of mind, not even after the two suicide attempts that I made while psychotic.

The suicidal person is asking, "Do I matter?" The best way to answer yes is to say it with action as well as with words. You may think you show it, and it should be obvious, but again, to articulate your love and concern is very powerful. Practice articulating your feelings so that when and if this test comes along, you will know better how to help save another person's life. Knowing what to do is just as important as knowing what to say.

What to Do

In line with not knowing what to say is not knowing what to do. If your relative or friend is behaving in an odd, out-of-character way, take the person to their doctor and/or the hospital and discuss the behavior you see, explaining to the person that you are concerned about the behavior you have seen him or her display. The person may simply need medication; don't be satisfied with a few placating words. Persist until the problem is uncovered and proper treatment is given.

Especially if he or she verbalizes a plan to suicide, right away without hesitation take this person to a hospital and do not settle for anything less than admission for your ill friend or relative. In any case, a person who is even thinking about killing themselves is in need of help. He or she needs family and friends to behave in a proactive, life-saving fashion.

In the Case of Psychosis: An Advocate is Especially Needed

With mental illness, the sufferer may not actually know that he or she is ill, as in the case of psychosis. For this reason, the ill one needs an advocate to come alongside, especially at this time, so the ill one can get the treatment he or she needs and deserves. The advocate can be a professional or a loved one or friend. It is so important not to dismiss the ill one as if he or she is fully responsible and in control of his or her own condition. Can a cancer patient make himself better? Should a person with "cancer of the mind" be expected to take full responsibility for themself?

It is important that the ill one embrace and try to be as proactive as possible in regard to his or her mental illness. Often such a one, if he or she is responsible, can take control and seek suitable treatment for themselves when they are well. It is particularly at the time of psychosis, however, that the ill one needs an advocate, because it is at those times that the illness can blind the mind of the sufferer as to the reality of his or her condition. If you as a loved one or friend become an advocate, be sure to educate yourself as to the signs and symptoms of psychosis with regard to the specific illness of the sufferer.

If you yourself suffer from a mental illness, I encourage you to try to articulate your struggles to a professional or to a loved one. Prepare for psychosis by choosing an advocate beforehand. It is sometimes very difficult to get admission. I know of people other than myself who experienced this. Take that person with you when you seek treatment, one who can help you insist that you receive the help you are asking for.

To the advocate: do not settle for anything less than what you feel the ill one needs. Do not be shy about expressing your concerns. Perseverance and assertion with an advocate can break through the barriers to treatment. I pray that you could help your friend or loved one, preventing him or her from acting on the suicidal ideation that can result from acute mental illness.

Remember that death is eternal. Death is a one-shot deal. The person with the illness can be fighting for his or her life. Unless that person has a battle plan, a firm understanding of the spiritual[1] nature of the war they are in, and an advocate, in my opinion, the illness can lead a person to act out on thoughts of self-harm. An advocate is so important, nay, necessary.

Perhaps if I had had a consistent advocate during my eleven month bout with psychosis and my persistent attempts to get help for myself, I may have been heard and my illness properly addressed without my having undergone a life-changing, catastrophic injury. I did go on occasion to the hospital with a few odd people, so even going once with someone may not get the ill one the proper treatment. That's why I so encourage persistence in regards to advocacy. Perhaps you as an advocate can prevent a tragedy from happening in the life of your loved one or friend through your consistent and persevering efforts.

When it comes to suicide, we would accept it from someone who is paralyzed. We could see physically the reason for their despair. But do we accept it as readily by someone who is mentally ill? We cannot readily see the root of their torment. Yet suicidal ideation is a symptom of acute mental illness and is a real killer.

Chapter 9: The Nature of "Suicidality" in Mental Illness

In my experience, the nature of "suicidality" in mental illness for me is that it can be felt as strongly as a need. Satan can cause suicidal tendencies to be felt like a need that can drive the person as strong as any other need, like the need for love, the need for food. It can consume a person and become like an addiction, especially in the case of repeat attempters.

Suicidal thoughts can become a panacea from the enormous pain of the illness. Contemplating suicide seriously can provide relief from a world that is fraught with the seemingly unending torment of mental illness. Satan tries to wear a person out with a constant barrage of emotional and spiritual pain. In the case of psychosis, this can be very exhausting, for it tends to take the person into another world, which is sometimes exciting but often terrifying.

I had been hearing voices when I was psychotic with delusions. These voices, for me, were condemning. They would say things like, "You're locked," "you're caught," "you're shot." I would actually believe these voices and let them guide me, thinking many of them were put there by God for Him to lead me into wellness.

Satan used this and my elaborate delusional world to wear me out. Satan used the health care professionals to whom I would go. The fact that they repeatedly turned me away from receiving the appropriate care that I needed caused the delusions to deepen—it caused me to believe, in my delusional state, that my problem was not psychiatric in nature, but that I was in fact a failure to God in His wonderful plan to heal me in a special way. As I've said, it was actually at the bridge that I believed that I was not getting better because of my own foolish choices. I decided at that time, that even going to the hospital seeking another admission was another foolish choice. Suicidality in mental illness can be the result of misinformation and confused thinking that can be present in the acute stages. If your mentally ill friend or relative is under the care of psychiatrist, and you still see symptoms in that person after some time, you may want to get a second opinion for your friend or relative.

Again, if illness is acute, don't be shy to take a proactive stance. We want to catch the ill one before he or she comes to a decision to act on a plan of suicide, because life is experienced by that person as not worth living. Impress upon the professionals the behavior you have observed and don't leave until the ill one gets the help that is satisfactory. Do not be satisfied with a little chat and some supportive conversation. The ill one's life may depend on it. Remember, suicidal ideation in the mentally ill can be felt as strongly as a need. Keen observation, protection, and advocacy is necessary with regard to dealing with one who is suicidal; I cannot stress this enough.

After a Suicide Attempt

We need to be careful to respond to those around us in love. Jesus says, "A new command I give you: Love one another. As I have loved you, so you must love one another. By this all men will know that you are my disciples, if you love one another."[1] If a loved one or friend has attempted suicide and survived, speak to that person about how you feel that he or she was not successful, affirming that person's worth and value in your life. It is not loving to avoid or ignore him or her using the excuse that you "don't know what to say."

Say something like, "I feel so sad that I couldn't help you before. I experienced guilt and loneliness, such helplessness when you tried to take your life. I can imagine these would be so amplified if you had succeeded. I cannot imagine my life with you forever gone from it. You are needed and valuable to me and of infinite preciousness to God and to the body of Christ. Your life means more than I can put into words. Please try to go on. I'll do what I can to help you."

We need to be reminded what love is: "Love is patient, love is kind ... it keeps no record of wrongs."[2] If you love this person, make a special effort to show the one who attempted suicide. Reaffirm the love you have by sharing from your heart with honesty and courage. I felt so much emptiness when I tried to take my life and people around me refused to address their feelings regarding the attempt.

Let your pain surrounding the attempt of your loved one spur you on to action to help that person find inner resources so that there would not be another attempt in the future. Forgive the person for hurting you by his or her attempting suicide. The one who has tried to kill himself or herself is crying out. Respond in love.

Don't be afraid to show the ill one this power-fully healing thing called love so he or she can find the strength to pick up, forgive themself (such a tough step), and carry on. Model forgiveness, deliver it first, so that the one who has attempted suicide can find strength to do it for themself.

Not Job—"I Will Never Forgive"

When Job lost his animals, his servants, his children, and his home, he

> fell to the ground in worship and said: 'Naked I came from my mother's womb, and naked I will depart. The LORD gave and the LORD has taken away; may the name of the LORD be praised.' In all this, Job did not sin by charging God with wrongdoing.[3]

He said this even when Satan was allowed to "strike his (Job's) flesh and bones."[4] The devil predicted that Job would then "curse (God) ... to his face."[5] Job even had his wife encouraging him not to hold on to his integrity and "(c)urse God and die."[6] Job's response to her was actually to call her "foolish."[7] He went on, "Shall we accept good from God and not trouble?"[8] Scripture says, "In all this, Job did not sin in what he said."[9]

My response was more than slightly different after my last suicide attempt, when Satan struck at my flesh and bones. Before the spinal cord injury, I would go on a prayer walk virtually every day. I had done this for years. I was also a swimmer, working out in the pool regularly, having been a lifeguard for over half my life.

It was mid-June 2002, about a year post-injury and about three months after I entered a long-term care facility. There I was confronted with no privacy, little quiet, and regularly interrupted sleep on an ongoing basis. I was not able to see beyond it, believing I would be there for the rest of my life. At that time, I wrote to God that I would "never forgive Him," that "I will always wish I had died at the foot of the Bloor St. Viaduct," that "this quality of life sucks," that I, in fact, "did not love Him."

Now, I am able to speak to individuals and groups about not giving up, about pressing on, and clinging to faith. I will again mention that the rough draft of this book was composed while I lived at this long-term care facility. I have my bad days, but I have generally come to a peace about the wheelchair, as God reveals to me that He is working in and through it.

Have you ever been in that place—where you believed the devil's lies that God cannot and will not grow you beyond your circumstances? I see them as just that— lies set to keep me in depression, to eradicate hope, and to distinguish the light of Jesus in my life. To reiterate, Satan's tactics are to get and keep us in despair so long, to torment us so much that it leads to our own destruction.

Remember the words of Isaiah:

> He gives strength to the weary and increases
> the power of the weak. Even youths grow tired
> and weary and young men stumble and fall; but
> those who hope in the LORD will renew their
> strength. They will soar on wings like eagles;
> they will run and not grow weary, they will walk
> and not be faint.[10]

This Scripture is full of promises. Did you catch that? I
believe this is speaking about a spiritual renewal, a spiritual soaring, running and walking.

Recall also Paul's words:

> And we rejoice in the hope of the glory of God.
> Not only so, but we also rejoice in our sufferings,
> because we know that suffering produces
> perseverance; perseverance, character; and
> character, hope. And hope does not disappoint
> us, because God has poured out his love into our
> hearts by the Holy Spirit, whom he has given
> us.[11]

It is so amazing that suffering is juxtaposed with the
word "hope" and with the idea that "God has poured out
his love into our hearts." Could it be that God is going to
accomplish this in and through your suffering, in a way
that He could not do any other way?

Paul goes on: "But God demonstrates his own love
for us in this: While we were still sinners, Christ died for
us."[12] Jesus paid the ultimate price for us. Willingly and
with courage He faced that which the Father laid before

Him. Can't we also learn from and emulate this example? Can we not face our "Gethsemanes" in the strength and power of Jesus to embrace that which God is asking us to endure? Or should we run? Just look at what the Father accomplished through the faithfulness and perseverance of Jesus!

Take heart, dear friend. As you look to Jesus with trust, He can change your inner cursing into shouts of joy with His blessings of strength and love showered into your heart. Notice that I did not speak here of "happiness," but of joy, as happiness is based on circumstances. Happiness comes and goes but joy persists even in and through difficult circumstances.

Joy is a fruit of the Spirit[13] that God can mold in any heart that is open and willing to endure the pruning. Jesus Himself said, "I am the true vine, and my Father is the gardener. He cuts off every branch in me that bears no fruit, while every branch that does bear fruit, he prunes so that it will be even more fruitful."[14] Endure the pruning, as Job did. Rail and curse if you must, as I did, just endure the pruning. On your Judgment Day, you will be eternally glad you did!

Chapter 10: The Power of Prayer

Despair is the very soil from which rich prayer can grow. A dwelling on negativity can actually nullify the power of prayer because it is exactly through dark emotions like despair that God calls us to reach to Him. God, if you will allow Him, will use your despair for His purposes. Allow Him to use it to teach you.

Jesus says, "Ask and it will be given to you; seek and you will find; knock and the door will be opened to you."[1] Again, notice the promises here. Charles Stanley says that these verbs in the original Greek were written in such an imperative form as to mean: ask and keep on asking, seek and keep on seeking, knock and keep on knocking. Be persistent, friend. Remember, "(S)eek and you *will* find" (italics mine).

Jesus looked to his disciples in the garden of Gethsemane, but found them sleeping. "'Could you men not keep watch with me for one hour?' he asked Peter. 'Watch and pray so that you will not fall into temptation. The spirit is willing but the body is weak.'"[2] Jesus knows the power of prayer to heal and to comfort, let alone the power in the petition itself. This is a warning that can be carried over to apply to those with suicidal thoughts or tendencies. Jesus calls us to pray to avoid falling into temptation. Our bodies can crave eternal rest, but it is the devil who tempts. "When tempted, no one should say, 'God is tempting me.' For God cannot be tempted by evil, nor does he tempt anyone."[3]

Again, in the garden of Gethsemane, Jesus himself prayed though in great pain. He said, "My soul is over-whelmed with sorrow to the point of death."[4] Jesus is not unacquainted with deep struggle; He knows what you are going through in your garden of Gethsemane. Won't you reach to Him? Won't you cry out to Him?

I was repeatedly having urinary tract infections or UTI's. I mentioned this to a prayer-warrior friend of mine, and she took it to the LORD. Unexplainable things started happening. Though infected, my bladder was behaving as if it was well. I was able, shortly thereafter, to report that I remained infection-free for much longer than I had ever been. I attribute all this to the power of prayer.

Some time thereafter I found, on sale, a bottle of vita-min C, 500 mg tablets. They didn't have the ones I usu-ally buy, the 250 mg size. So I bought the larger pills and started using them, taking two a day, along with my cranberry capsules of which I also take two a day. Low and behold, I didn't have a bladder infection for about ten months, whereas before, I was just recovering from a UTI only to get another one very soon afterward! This regi-men is indeed an answer to prayer, because I was becom-ing increasingly resistant to antibiotics. I just stumbled upon this combination of pills, as I said. Surely there are no coincidences with God.

Lift up your issues to Him who cares for you. Get others to do this as well, and watch God work as you feel your helplessness drain from you. All the issues over which you have no control you can pray about. That's one way to take power back. Give up control for the situation to Him who knows all and has the power to remedy it, should He choose to do so. Just know that His activity or seeming inactivity following prayer is completely up to Him, remembering that He is, at His core, mystery.

We All Need Help

Certainly, deep help and solace can come through prayer. Indeed, we all need help, at certain times more than at others. In the garden of Gethsemane, even Jesus reached both vertically and horizontally. The Bible says that He went with His disciples to the garden and specifically asked Peter and the two sons of Zebedee to "(s)tay here and keep watch with me."[5] Then, looking up, "(H)e fell with his face to the ground and spoke to the Father, asking Him, 'If it is possible, may this cup be taken from me.'"[6]

Then Jesus turned and went back to His disciples, finding that they had not kept watch as He had asked. After speaking to them, the horizontal, Jesus returns to the Father, the vertical, and prays again, "(Y)our will be done."[7]

He then makes His way back to the disciples to find them asleep again, then returns to the Father. Finally,

He goes once again to the disciples to speak to them. Notice Jesus modeling this back-and-forth movement for us when He is "overwhelmed with sorrow to the point of death."[8] When we are in great pain, we, as did Jesus, need people around us to help us. Especially when we are deeply sorrowful, we need supportive people around us who can help us.

For me, I go to Christ in prayer, and I also go to my advisers, my counselor, and my supportive friends and family. Back and forth I go, especially in times of deep distress.

Jesus, through this process, developed the strength to be able to say to His Father, "(Y)et not as I will, but as you will."[9] If you are feeling or have felt like life is not worth living, know that if God wanted you in heaven with Him, He could take you. You are here for a reason. If Jesus gave up in His garden of Gethsemane, we would not have the Savior of the world.

God wants to use you in your pain as He did with Jesus in pain; perhaps He wants to make you a small "s" savior in His plan to bring others to Himself, to comfort and encourage others as they see His strength and light in you. Won't you look to Him and let Him give you the strength to pray, "Yet not as I will, but as you will"? If Jesus, who was 100% divine as well as 100% human, needed help, how much more do we as mere mortals need it? Let God be God in your life; look to omnipotence and to others interdependently, for we all need help.

Chapter 11: Going On is Tougher

I knew an older woman who was paralyzed from the waist down. She was also partially blind and deaf and lived in the institution. She tried to starve herself to death. What turned her around was her grandchild saying, "What kind of an example are you setting for us, Grandma?"

I said to her that taking your life takes great courage. She said, "Going on is tougher." Choose the tougher road; trust God and watch him give you "a crown of beauty instead of ashes ..."[1]

The Two Great Commandments

Life may be tough but we have commandments to guide us and strengthen us. Jesus said that the "most important"[2] and "the first and greatest"[3] commandment is to "Love the LORD your God with all your heart and with all your soul and with all your mind and with all your strength."[4] Love involves trust, and trust involves faith. We need to reach out in love and have trust and faith that

God, in His sovereign wisdom, seeing things as He does from an eternal perspective, knows what He is doing by allowing our suffering.

The "second"⁵ greatest commandment is this: "Love your neighbour as yourself," which appears numerous times in the New Testament: Matthew 19:19; Mark 12:31; Luke 10:27; Romans 13:9; Galatians 5:14; James 2:8. As I have said, there are two commands here: to love your neighbor and also to love yourself. Suicide is called, "hurting yourself;" it is not loving yourself. It may feel like suicide is an act of loving yourself because you think it will get you out of your pain, but feelings are changeable. It is unwise to act on feelings.

Besides, if you do not have a personal relationship with Christ when you die, either by your own hand or not, you will suffer inescapably and eternally in a much graver, much more painful state than you can imagine. Any suffering here on earth does not compare with facing an eternity in hell. Living in an institution and being displaced from your home may be a taste of hell, but it does not compare to the actual place.

Loving the LORD and loving yourself are paramount in accepting Jesus Christ as your personal Savior. It is a sign of healthy self-love to acknowledge your inadequacy in yourself and your subsequent need of a Savior.

Jesus said: "I tell you the truth, no one can see the kingdom of God unless he is born again (or born from above)."⁶ What is necessary is a spiritual rebirth. Jesus also made the claim, "I am the way and the truth and the life. No one comes to the Father except through me."⁷ He is either telling the truth or He is a liar. You decide.

If you have not already done so, just say with your

heart, "Dear Jesus, I know I do wrong things. Please forgive me of my sins. Come into my heart and be my LORD and Savior. Help me to serve you and obey you. In Jesus' name. Amen."

If you have prayed that prayer with your heart, congratulations, you are now a blood-bought child of God! Jesus says, "I tell you, there is rejoicing in the presence of the angels of God over one sinner who repents."[8]

When you pray a prayer like the one above, when God the Father looks at you, He no longer sees the sin that He cannot accept but His Son. He can, therefore, admit you into His Holy Heaven, since He cannot abide by sin. I encourage you to tell someone if you prayed that prayer: a pastor, a Christian friend, or a Christian organization that can help you in your walk with Christ. Saying this prayer is just the beginning of a beautiful relationship with Christ. You need now, to be discipled to understand how to walk in the Spirit and live daily for Jesus.

Turning to God in such a prayer though, as I've said, is a way in which we can love ourselves. All Christ-centered prayer is, in fact, central to loving ourselves and loving God. Though God's salvation is a gift of grace,[9] God seems, however, to require of us much work just to maintain stability. I understand that we get very tired.

Fatigue

Fatigue can be an indication that something is wrong with your body, that you are, in fact, ill. But it can also be used by the enemy, the devil, to deceive. It can be a barrier to doing good works.

Sometimes we can feel an almost unsatiated exhaustion. There are times when I feel downright tormented by fatigue. I awake in the morning, grasping in my mind at a time during the day in which I can take a nap. The medication I'm on causes drowsiness and contributes to this, however. Seems sometimes, as if the more we give in to fatigue, though, the more our bodies can crave rest. We go on "vacations" only to come home and feel like we need to rest up afterwards.

I believe that we must fight this tendency if we are to consistently accomplish good works. I find I can go on less sleep than I imagined. Able-bodied, I used to get upset when I was woken from my sleep. In the institution, I was woken regularly at 3 a.m. to empty my bladder and sometimes at other times in the night because of the noise of the nurses. I went to sleep often not until after 11:30 p.m. and would rise at 6:30 a.m. because of noise due to shift changes. Seven hours of interrupted sleep may not seem too bad to you, but I believed I required about nine hours to function well.

When I was able-bodied, I used to sleep for twelve hours once a week, believing that I needed it. Sometimes what we think we need in terms of sleep and what we actually need is vastly different. It takes sometimes an eye-opening occurrence to help us tell the difference. For me, it was the paralysis and living in the institution that did it.

Nowadays, I feel energized by joy. Truly, "the joy of the LORD is ... (my) strength."[10] I experience such intense spiritual freedom that I can claim this verse in Nehemiah. There are times, though, when I feel burdened and upset with the paralysis. I have my bad days, as I've said, when the blues come knocking and fatigue tempts me to retreat. I believe that this is just part of the natural ebb and flow of life as on a beach with the tide coming in and receding. But when fatigue threatens to eat up my time and my efforts at a good work, when I'm tempted to stay home from church, I remember the verse which I have quoted earlier: "For our struggle is not against flesh and blood, but against the rulers, against the authorities, against the powers of this dark world and against the spiritual forces of evil in the heavenly realms."[11] Paul goes on to tell us what to do: "Therefore, put on the full armor of God, so that when the day of evil comes, you may be able to stand your ground, and after you have done everything, to stand."[12]

This verse is proof that we are in a war! When I feel the enemy tempting me to retreat and back down, I think of these verses—that all I need to do is stand in the face of an attack. Scripture tells us: "A little sleep, a little slumber, a little folding of the hands to rest—and poverty will come on you like a bandit and scarcity like an armed man."[13] Frequently, I am left with a choice to get "suited up" in the armor and stay in the fight or give in and retreat.

When I am facing unreasonable fatigue, for example, fatigue that is there that has no physical cause or reason, I am aware that it may certainly be the devil who is tempting. I might recite some Scripture such as: "(T)he one who is in (me) ... is greater than the one who is in the world,"[14] or "He who began a good work in (me) ... will carry it on to completion until the day of Christ Jesus."[15] The joy inevitably comes flooding back as the enemy backs off.

Again, fatigue can deceive and eat up quality time. It can make you believe that you can't make it, that you can't play that game with the kids, that you can't do that extra report, that you can't engage in that heart-to-heart that someone was asking of you, that you can't do the work of unpacking your feelings about a troubling situation in therapy, that you can't pray or read the Bible. How often have you fallen asleep praying?

I often admire my former psychologist at the rehab hospital for people with spinal cord injuries; he is such a master at pushing beyond his fatigue. He could, after a long day at work, find the time and energy for a whole hour with me just because I asked. He was not in the least bit irritated or frustrated. He was merely forthright; he would tell me if he could do it. His behavior was so helpful, especially because I was often treated with impatience from the adults whom I looked to for support when I was growing up. The "greatness" in an individual is tested and seen, I believe, when one seeks the strength that is ultimately given by God, and is, consequently, able to push beyond fatigue and produce despite it, without complaint.

We need to be wise when it comes to fatigue if we are to consistently accomplish good works. Fatigue, though, can be a gauge. It can be a necessary and helpful one at that. It can signal illness, as I've said. Perhaps it could be telling us that we are "burning the candle at both ends" or demanding more of ourselves than is healthy.

If this is the case with you, remember Jesus' words:

> Come to me, all who are weary and burdened,
> and I will give you rest. Take my yoke upon you

and learn from me, for I am gentle and humble
in heart, and you will find rest for your souls.
For my yoke is easy and my burden is light.[16]

He alone can exchange your heaviness with lightness and
joy from His heart to yours. Certainly there is a time
for rest and for play, and a time for work and for facing
fatigue: "There is a time for everything, and a season for
every activity under heaven."[17]

I do not mean to discount fatigue that is good and
that triggers a problem. However, I find it unsurprising
that when I am about to set out to accomplish a good
work for God, Satan throws fatigue at me. Have you had
that experience? I found the last few courses in the cur-
riculum when I was studying to be the most arduous of
all that I had done in the three years of the degree. Satan
knew that I was about to complete a good work for God,
so he put the barrier of fatigue in my path.

Chapter 12: Some Relevant Scripture—Part 1

I used to think that the Bible was silent about suicide. I have even heard biblical scholars say this. But I am finding that there are numerous exhortations to go on. Take these as examples (my list here is not in the least exhaustive):

Galatians 6:9: "Let us not become weary in doing good, for at the proper time we will reap a harvest if we do not give up."

2 Chronicles 15:7: "But as for you, be strong and do not give up, for your work will be rewarded."

2 Corinthians 1:8–11:

> We do not want you to be uninformed, brothers, about the hardships we suffered in the province of Asia. We were under great pressure, far beyond our ability to endure, so that we despaired even of life. Indeed, in our hearts we felt the sentence of death. But this happened that we might not rely on ourselves but on God, who raises the dead. He has delivered us from such a deadly

peril, and he will deliver us. On him we have
set our hope that he will continue to deliver us,
as you help us by your prayers. Then many will
give thanks on our behalf for the gracious favor
granted us in answer to the prayers of many.

The suffering unto death had a purpose: "(T)hat we
might not rely on ourselves but on God, who raises the
dead." Certainly if He can raise the dead, He can handle
your problems, Paul seems to say here. Note the promises
here: He "will deliver us" and He "will continue to deliver
us." Notice also that prayers help the sufferers.

2 Corinthians 4:13–18:

> It is written: 'I believed; therefore I have spoken.'
> With that same spirit of faith we also believe and
> therefore speak, because we know that the one
> who raised the LORD Jesus from the dead will
> also raise us with Jesus and present us with you in
> his presence. All this is for your benefit, so that
> the grace that is reaching more and more people
> may cause thanksgiving to overflow to the glory
> of God. Therefore we do not lose heart. Though
> outwardly we are wasting away, yet inwardly we
> are being renewed day by day. For our light and
> momentary troubles are achieving for us an
> eternal glory that far outweighs them all. So we
> fix our eyes not on what is seen, but on what is
> unseen. For what is seen is temporary, but what
> is unseen is eternal.

Notice the similarities to the previous verse I have quoted:
"we know that the one who raised the LORD Jesus from

the dead will also raise us with Jesus". Again, Paul speaks of purposes in suffering that "grace … may cause thanksgiving to overflow to the glory of God", that "inwardly we are being renewed day by day", that our "troubles are achieving for us an eternal glory that far outweighs them all". So we are to "fix our eyes" on the eternal Jesus.

Jesus in Luke 9:23: "If anyone would come after me, he must deny himself and take up his cross daily and follow me." It is a struggle that is meant to be taken in day chunks.

2 John 8: "Watch out that you do not lose what you have worked for, but that you may be rewarded fully." Remember how hard you have worked to get to where you are today, and how patient and loving God has been along the way.

Prayer is linked to despair. "Jesus told his disciples a parable to show them that they should always pray and not give up."[1] Jesus then goes on to divulge the Parable of the Persistent Widow who hounds an unjust judge with her petitions. The judge relents finally, saying,

> 'Even though I don't fear God or care about men, yet because this widow keeps bothering me, I will see that she gets justice, so that she won't eventually wear me out with her coming!' And the LORD said, 'Listen to what the unjust judge says. And will not God bring about justice for his chosen ones, *who cry out to him day and night?* Will he keep putting them off? I tell you, he will see that they get justice, and quickly.'[2] (italics mine).

Perhaps, you will not see "human justice" in this realm, but come your Judgment Day, you surely will, if you hold fast to Jesus.

To further illustrate the connection between despair and prayer, I point to the place where Jesus said to his disciples, in the garden of Gethsemane, "Watch and pray so that you will not fall into temptation. The spirit is willing but the body is weak."[3] Jesus knows your weakness and therefore, urges you to pray.

Deuteronomy 31:6,7,23; Joshua 1:6,7,9,18; 10:25; 1 Chronicles 22:13; 28:20; 2 Chronicles 32:7: "Be strong and courageous."

Philippians 4:11–13:

> I have learned to be content whatever the circumstances. I know what it is to be in need and I know what it is to have plenty. I have learned the secret of being content in any and every situation, whether well fed or hungry, whether living in plenty or in want. I can do everything through him who gives me strength" (written by Paul from a prison).

Jesus in Matthew 11:28–30: "Come to me, all you who are weary and burdened, and I will give you rest. Take my yoke upon you and learn from me, for I am gentle and humble in heart, and you will find rest for your souls. For my yoke is easy and my burden is light."

Romans 5:2b-4: "And we rejoice in the hope of the glory of God. Not only so but we also rejoice in our sufferings, because we know that suffering produces perseverance; perseverance, character; and character, hope."

Romans 7:15–25:

> I do not understand what I do. For what I want
> to do I do not do, but what I hate I do. And if
> I do what I do not want to do, I agree that the
> law is good. As it is, it is no longer I myself
> who do it, but it is sin living in me. I know that
> nothing good lives in me, that is, in my sinful
> nature. For I have the desire to do what is good,
> but I cannot carry it out. For what I do is not
> the good I want to do; no, the evil I do not want
> to do—this I keep on doing. Now if I do what
> I do not want to do, it is no longer I who do it,
> but it is sin living in me that does it. So I find
> this law at work: When I want to do good, evil
> is right there with me. For in my inner being I
> delight in God's law; but I see another law at
> work in the members of my body, waging war
> against the law of my mind and making me a
> prisoner of the law of sin at work within my
> members. What a wretched man I am! Who
> will rescue me from this body of death? Thanks
> be to God—through Jesus Christ our LORD!

Indeed it is only Christ who "rescue(s)" any of us in this
war we are all in!

Romans 12:1–2:

> I urge you, brothers, in view of God's mercy, to
> offer your bodies as living (as opposed to dead)
> sacrifices, holy and pleasing to God—this is
> your spiritual act of worship. Do not conform
> any longer to the pattern of this world, but be

transformed by the renewing of your mind. Then you will be able to test and approve what God's will is—his good, pleasing and perfect will (amplification mine).

Romans 12:21: "Do not be overcome by evil, but overcome evil with good."

1 Corinthians 7:19: "*Keeping* God's commands is what counts" (italics mine).

1 Peter 4:12–13:

> Dear friends, do not be surprised at the painful trial you are suffering as though something strange were happening to you. But rejoice that you participate in the sufferings of Christ, so that you may be overjoyed when his glory is revealed.

Certainly Jesus promised that we would have trouble[4]; what is important is our attitude, as I outlined earlier.

Some Relevant Scripture—Part 2

Emotions: Fear, Anger, Anxiety

Isaiah 35:4; 41:13: 43:1: "Do not fear".

Isaiah 41:10: "So do not fear, for I am with you; do not be dismayed, for I am your God. I will strengthen you and help you; I will uphold you with my righteous right hand."

Psalm 56:3–4: "When I am afraid, I will trust in you. In God, whose word I praise, in God I trust; I will not be afraid. What can mortal man do to me?"

Psalm 118:6–7: "The LORD is with me; I will not be afraid. What can man do to me? The LORD is with me; he is my helper, I will look in triumph on my enemies."

Isaiah 12:2: "Surely God is my salvation; I will trust and not be afraid. The LORD, the LORD, is my strength and my song".

Jesus in Mark 5:36: "Don't be afraid; just believe."

Jesus in John 14:27: "Do not let your hearts be troubled and do not be afraid."

Proverbs 8:13: "To fear the LORD is to hate evil; I hate pride and arrogance, evil behavior and perverse speech."

Ephesians 4:26: "'In your anger do not sin': Do not let the sun go down while you are still angry, and do not give the devil a foothold."

1 Peter 5:7: "Cast all your anxiety on him, because he cares for you."

Philippians 4:6–7:

> "Do not be anxious about anything, but in everything, by prayer and petition, with thanksgiving, present your requests to God. And the peace of God, which transcends all understanding, will guard your hearts and your minds in Christ Jesus."

When I was in the institution, I read this as if it were a formula for peace. I have found since that this is the case, that this verse is indeed true; it is a promise that is totally reliable.

Perseverance passages

Jesus in Luke 8:15: The Parable of the Sower concludes
with these words: "But the seed on good soil stands for
those with a noble and good heart, who hear the word,
retain it, and by *persevering* produce a crop" (italics
mine).

Jesus in John 8:31–32: "If you *hold* to my teaching, you
are really my disciples. Then you will know the truth, and
the truth will set you free" (italics mine).

1 Corinthians 13:7: "(Love) always protects, always
trusts, always hopes, always perseveres."

Hebrews 10:36–39:

> "You need to persevere so that when you have
> done the will of God, you will receive what he
> has promised. For in just a very little while, 'He
> who is coming will come and will not delay. But
> my righteous one will live by faith. And if he
> shrinks back, I will not be pleased with him.'
> But we are not of those who shrink back and
> are destroyed, but of those who believe and are
> saved."

Commentaries on this passage seem to be saying that
we are in need of patience and perseverance. That it is
through these things that we are able to firmly and constantly advance.

Hebrews 11:27: "By faith, he (Moses) left Egypt, not
fearing the king's anger; he persevered because he saw
him who is invisible." By faith, Moses experienced the

living God and was able to keep going because he "saw him who is invisible."

James 1:12: "Blessed is the man who perseveres under trial, because when he has stood the test, he will receive the crown of life that God has promised to those who love him."

James 5:11: "As you know, we consider blessed those who have persevered. You have heard of Job's perseverance and have seen what the LORD finally brought about. The LORD is full of compassion and mercy."

Jesus in Revelation 2:2a-3: "I know your deeds, your hard work and your perseverance... . You have persevered and have endured hardships for my name." Rest assured that God knows.

Chapter 13: More Relevant Scripture

"Faithful"

Deuteronomy 7:9: "Know ... that the LORD your God is God; he is the faithful God, keeping his covenant of love to a thousand generations of those who love him and keep his commands."

2 Samuel 22:26–27, Psalm 18:25–26: "To the faithful you (LORD) show yourself faithful, to the blameless you show yourself blameless, to the pure you show yourself pure, but to the crooked you show yourself shrewd."

Psalm 31:23b-24: "The LORD preserves the faithful, but the proud he pays back in full. Be strong and take heart, all you who hope in the LORD."

Psalm 33:4: "For the word of the LORD is right and true; he is faithful in all he does."

Psalm 145:13b: "The LORD is faithful to all his promises and loving toward all he has made."

Proverbs 2:7–8: "He holds victory in store for the

upright, he is a shield to those whose walk is blameless, for he guards the course of the just and protects the way of his faithful ones."

We do so desire to hear these words in Matthew 25:21, 23: "Well done, good and faithful servant!"

Romans 12:12: "Be joyful in hope, patient in affliction, faithful in prayer."

1 Corinthians 1:9: "He will keep you strong to the end, so that you will be blameless on the day of our LORD Jesus Christ. God, who has called you into fellowship with his Son Jesus Christ our LORD, is faithful."

1 Thessalonians 5:24: "The one who calls you is faithful and he will do it."

2 Thessalonians 3:3: "But the LORD is faithful and he will strengthen and protect you from the evil one."

Hebrews 3:6: "But Christ is faithful as a son over God's house. And we are his house, if we hold on to our courage and the hope of which we boast."

Hebrews 10:23–24: "Let us hold unswervingly to the hope we profess, for he who promised is faithful. And let us consider how we may spur one another on toward love and good deeds." Attempting suicide will not "spur one another on toward love and good deeds." In fact, it may result in someone else attempting suicide. I refer you here to my poem, *Contagious*.

Jesus in Revelation 2:10: "Be faithful, even to the point of death, and I will give you the crown of life."

More on "Rewards"

1 Samuel 26:23: "The LORD rewards every man for his righteousness and faithfulness."

Psalm 19:11: "By them (the ordinances of the LORD) is your servant warned; in keeping them there is great reward."

Psalm 62:13b: "Surely you will reward each person according to what he has done."

Proverbs 11:18: "The wicked man earns deceptive wages, but he who sows righteousness reaps a sure reward."

Proverbs 25:21–22: "If your enemy is hungry, give him food to eat; if he is thirsty, give him water to drink. In doing this, you will heap burning coals on his head, and the LORD will reward you."

Jeremiah 17:10: "'I the LORD search the heart and examine the mind, to reward a man according to his conduct, according to what his deeds deserve.'"

Jeremiah 32:19b: "Your eyes are open to all the ways of men; you reward everyone according to his conduct and as his deeds deserve."

Matthew 5:11–12:

> "Blessed are you when people insult you, persecute you and falsely say all kinds of evil against you because of me. Rejoice and be glad, because great is your reward in heaven, for in the same way they persecuted the prophets who were before you."

Jesus in Matthew 16:27: "For the Son of Man is going to

come in his Father's glory with his angels, and then he will reward each person according to what he has done."

Luke 6:35: "But love your enemies, do good to them, and lend to them without expecting to get anything back. Then your reward will be great".

Ephesians 6:7–8: "Serve wholeheartedly, as if you were serving the LORD, not men, because you know that the LORD will reward everyone for whatever good he does, whether he is slave or free."

Jesus in Revelation 22:12: "Behold, I am coming soon! My reward is with me, and I will give to everyone according to what he has done."

"Stand Firm"

Ephesians 6:10–14a:

> "Finally, be strong in the LORD and in his mighty power. Put on the full armor of God so that you can take your stand against the devil's schemes. For our struggle is not against flesh and blood, but against the rulers, against the authorities, against the powers of this dark world and against the spiritual forces of evil in the heavenly realms. Therefore put of the full armor of God, so that when the day of evil comes, you may be able to stand your ground and after you have done everything, to stand. Stand firm then ..."

Verse 10, "Be(ing) strong in the LORD and in his mighty power", to me, means laying my burdens down at the foot of the cross and leaving them there, firmly standing and surrendering my pain. I say as I do this, "You fight for me. It is too big for me. I need you to do it, Jesus." I'm reminded here of certain other verses, some of which I've mentioned earlier, like: "(T)he battle is the LORD's"[1]; "For the battle is not yours, but God's"[2]; and, "The LORD will fight for you"[3]. I then ask God to "suit me up" and help me to "stand", as is outlined in Ephesians 6:10–14a, as that is my responsibility, letting God be God in my life and letting Him fight for me.

1 Peter 5:8–9:

> "Be self-controlled and alert. Your enemy the devil prowls around like a roaring lion looking for someone to devour. Resist him, standing firm in the faith, because you know that your brothers throughout the world are undergoing the same kind of sufferings."

Waiting Scriptures

Psalm 27:13–14: "I am still confident of this: I will see the goodness of the LORD in the land of the living. Wait for the LORD; be strong and take heart and wait for the LORD."

Psalm 40:1–2: "I waited patiently for the LORD; he turned to me and heard my cry. He lifted me out of the slimy pit, out of the mud and mire; he set my feet on a rock and gave me a firm place to stand."

Psalm 130:5: "I wait for the LORD, my soul waits and in his word I put my hope."

Isaiah 30:18: "Yet the LORD longs to be gracious to you; he rises to show you compassion. For the LORD is a God of justice. Blessed are all who wait for him!"

Isaiah 64:4: "Since ancient times no one has heard, no ear has perceived, no eye has seen any God besides you, who acts on behalf of those who wait for him."

Jesus to his disciples in Acts 1:4: "(W)ait for the gift my Father promised".

The Scriptures speak of "patient endurance"[4].

Romans 8:22–25:

> "We know that the whole creation has been groaning as in the pains of childbirth right up to the present time. Not only so, but we ourselves, who have the firstfruits of the Spirit, groan inwardly as we wait eagerly for our adoption as sons, the redemption of our bodies. For to this hope we were saved. But hope that is seen is no hope at all. Who hopes for what he already has? But if we hope for what we do not yet have, we wait for it patiently."

Philippians 1:6: "(B)eing confident of this, that he who began a good work in you will carry it on to completion until the day of Christ Jesus."

One caution: Scripture is "God-breathed."[5] Yet as we can see when we read about the temptations of Christ by Satan, the devil readily quoted Scripture:

> "Then the devil took him to the holy city and had him stand on the highest point of the temple. 'If

you are the Son of God,' he said, 'throw yourself down. For it is written: 'He will command his angels concerning you, and they will lift you up in their hands, so that you will not strike your foot against a stone'"[6]. (This last verse which the devil quoted is taken from Psalm 91:11–12.)

In my first suicide attempt, Satan gave me the verse, "I can do everything through him (Christ) who gives me strength"[7] as I cut myself. The best way I know to ensure that Christ is in fact giving you Scripture is to test the spirits as laid out in 1 John 4:1–3:

> "Dear friends, do not believe every spirit, but test the spirits to see whether they are from God, because many false prophets have gone out into the world. This is how you can recognize the Spirit of God: Every spirit that acknowledges that Jesus Christ has come in the flesh is from God, but every spirit that does not acknowledge Jesus is not from God. This is the spirit of the antichrist, which you have heard is coming and even now is already in the world."

I simply address the spirit that is influencing me and ask, "Do you proclaim Jesus as LORD?" I sense a response: either "Yes" or "No". "Yes" means that the original response was from God. "No" means that the devil is up to his old tricks.

When approaching Scripture, it is also appropriate to ask God and God only to speak to you, that the Holy Spirit would lead you to and illumine that portion of the Word that He wants you to read.

On Waiting

The Second Coming of Christ is certain, yet: "No one
knows about that day or hour, not even the angels in
heaven, nor the Son, but only the Father ... Therefore
keep watch, because you do not know on what day your
LORD will come."[8] I keep this in the back of my mind
that at any time I could be relieved of my cross and be
taken up with him. This encourages me to live in a godly
fashion, pleasing to the LORD. It also gives me hope and
strength.

Paul puts it this way:

> For the grace of God that brings salvation has
> appeared to all men. It teaches us to say 'No'
> to ungodliness and worldly passions, and to
> live self-controlled, upright and godly lives in
> this present age, while we wait for the blessed
> hope—the glorious appearing of our great God
> and Savior, Jesus Christ, who gave himself for us
> to redeem us from all wickedness and to purify
> for himself a people that are his very own, eager
> to do what is good.[9]

We need to "keep watch" and wait not only for the Second
Coming but also for the possibility of a miracle from
Jesus. Jesus himself speaks of "the miracles I do in my
Father's name."[10] These are also Jesus' words: "The blind
receive sight, the lame walk, those who have leprosy are
cured, the deaf hear, the dead are raised and good news
is preached to the poor. Blessed is the man who does not
fall away on account of me."[11]

I reiterate here that we need to keep Jesus' miracle-working power in mind and wait in watchful hope that He may choose to do a miraculous healing. He has definitely performed miracles in my heart redeeming me from depression after depression. Certainly, He delivered me from delusions, even though he has not as yet chosen to heal my paralysis.

Perhaps, looking back, you can see God's faithful hand in delivering you. Certainly, God has saved us time and again from situations we know nothing about but will know one day. It's important to sit down in times of hardship and wait on Him, allowing God to recount all the times that He has helped us. Let yourself wait in hopeful anticipation for the Second Coming of Christ and His miraculous healing power, allowing these realities to give you strength and hope for today.

Chapter 14: Self Esteem

Over four decades of life, including years of counseling and spiritual direction, and I still, at my core, wonder why when a man is attracted to me, especially now that I'm in the wheelchair. I've received significant healing from where I was in my early years, but I will say that it's very difficult to counter totally the effects of an upbringing that held much turmoil. Just as the sin of one man, Adam, had such a pervasive effect on humanity, so the mistreatment of a child can damage and scar that person to some degree for life.

My mother and father, much as they tried, were unable to affirm and to show consistent love and discipline when I was a youngster. This, at least in part, left me feeling unworthy, unworthy of attention, and unworthy of being fought for. At least partially because of this low self-esteem, when life circumstances heated up, when things got very tough, I was unable to withstand the stress because my internal architecture, the foundation, was not strong. I tended to spiral into negativity. That's why I talk about a predisposition to suicide.

Suicidal Predisposition? Part 1

It's a curious phenomenon when, under the same or very similar stress, one person becomes suicidal and the other is able to press on, to endure. One situation pushes one person past the brink of despair, whereas another person undergoing the same or very similar stress is able to persevere, perhaps without suicidal ideation at all.

This is a curious phenomenon. With me, there was the development of mental illness. Certainly suicidal ideation can be a symptom of acute mental illness. (I do know, however, of some with mental illness who do not become suicidal in acute crisis.) I was able to develop a healthy support system outside my immediate family comprised of counselors and friends as I faced the fact that I was not going to find the strongest emotional support that I craved from my family of origin. I learned over the years to relate interdependently to my supports. I was able to find significant healing for deep childhood wounds. And I eventually found the right balance of psychiatric medication with the help of good psychiatrists.

Fundamentally, in regards to a remedy to suicidal ideation, the base line is drawn in the ability to trust and seek God. I know of a Christian song that says, "It's not in trying but in trusting. It's not in running but in resting. It's not in wondering but in praying, that we find the strength of the LORD." When we try and when we run and when we wonder, we exert our own strength. When we trust, we look to Him. When we rest in faith, He carries us. When we pray, we find intimacy with the Almighty.

The enemy tries to turn us away from God by getting us to place our gaze on our circumstances instead of on our Creator. As we fix our eyes on Him, our circumstances diminish and He increases. He gives us the strength we need when we trust and seek Him with all our hearts.

From an early age, I had a sense that "I am me," and felt that I was the only one upon whom I could truly rely or depend. When I became paralyzed and was thrust into a situation where I needed people on a daily basis to perform even basic bodily functions, I struggled deeply. For some years I wrestled with this.

Then it came to me that I was not in the hands of anyone else but the Almighty God. I truly needed to believe that, "in all things God works for the good of those who love him, who have been called according to his purpose."[1] In doing so, I truly had nothing to fear; not even despair itself was reason to fear. All God was asking of me was trust.

God used the vehicle of trust to bring me through the despair of helplessness and empower me to find independence to such a degree that I never thought possible in the early days of my paralysis. He used my broken family to support and provide; we are now closer than we have ever been. It strikes me that able-bodied or disabled, we all need to be dependent on God, to trust Him, and in doing so, learn to relate to each other interdependently.

I found that I tended towards sadness and negativity because that felt "comfortable" for me, that "fit who I was," I felt. When I became a Christian and experienced the joy of the LORD, my countenance lifted. As I grew more accustomed to having joy in my life, I tended to lean more and more on Christ and spent less time in negativity and sadness. I found that as I allowed Christ to permeate my spirit, others were attracted to that joy and it was easier to build up a healthy social network for myself.

Jesus had his twelve disciples. As I mentioned, in the garden of Gethsemane, Jesus Himself went interchangeably to His friends and to His Father. He went to them in a back-and-forth movement in his period of deep stress and crisis. Having a network of support for yourself is so important; when we encounter our Gethsemanes, we too can enlist the support of caring others as well as the caring Father. And it is this that can keep us from acting on the tendencies toward suicidal ideation if, in fact, we suffer from a suicidal predisposition, something I believe is real.

I feel that I developed a suicidal predisposition in part because I lived in a deep, depressed place as a child and did not experience the strengths and joys of a functional family unit, and in part because I was unable to have a healthy dependence and bond with my parents in my early years. With the strong tension between them since I was four years old, I was not able to bond properly with either one of them as I felt their overt disdain for one another. Having witnessed an altercation between my parents also at age four, I developed unhealthy fears of them instead of trust, which carried over to my feelings for other people, and indeed for God. In addition, my mother relied on her girls, my older sister and I, for support; she herself did not have many friends and I believe had not yet learned to relate to people interdependently. In light of these circumstances, I could not be expected to develop socially in a healthy way.

I became suicidal so frequently and so easily partly because of the presence of mental illness, partly because of my fear-hearted nature, partly because I found this life so difficult with few real joys but mostly I believe because I had not been modeled or fully grasped the fundamental truth of Ephesians 6:12, that we are in a spiritual war.

I restate Ephesians 6:10–13 to put verse 12 in context:

> Finally, be strong in the LORD and in his mighty power. Put on the full armor of God so that you can take your stand against the devil's schemes. For our struggle is not against flesh and blood, but against the rulers, against the authorities, against the powers of this dark world and against the spiritual forces of evil in the heavenly realms. Therefore put on the full armor of God, so that when the day of evil comes, you may be able to stand your ground, and after you have done everything, to stand.

I repeat this verse often to stress the point that we are all in a war of a spiritual nature, not with people as we may suspect at first glance. It is Satan who tempts a person to suicide.

Having experienced scapegoating from a young age, as well as parentification, having witnessed ongoing deep hostility from both my parents, these experiences laid a foundation of mistrust and fear in childhood, that at least, in part, made me more prone to negativity. These things caused me to tend to give in to the power of the enemy in the war again that we all fight. However, had I fully come to the simple understanding that it was the devil tempting me to self-harm, I think I would have been able to resist. I know now that I need to lean just more intensely on Christ when Satan is testing my faith and tempting me to self-destruction.

Rick Warren says in his book, *The Purpose Driven Life*, that character is both developed and revealed by tests, that all of life is, in fact, a test. He says that you are always being tested. God constantly watches your response, reveals Warren, to people, problems, success, conflict, illness, disappointment, and even the weather.

God calls us to the vertical and to the horizontal, to Himself, and to the body of believers, just as He modeled for us in the Garden of Gethsemane as I have outlined earlier. It is only Jesus who can break through the walls, the barriers of fear and self-loathing that can result from negativity encountered in a dysfunctional family upbringing; it is He who encourages a healthy dependence on Himself and subsequent interdependence with others. When our first relationships are insecure and not consistently modeling the love that ultimately comes from Christ, we can find it difficult to achieve and maintain a relationship to God. I will explain more about how this works in the next part.

Chapter 15: Suicidal Predisposition? Part 2

As I've said, when our first relationships were insecure and not consistently modeling Christ's love, we can find it difficult to achieve and maintain a relationship to God. For me, my feelings for my father and mother were transferred onto God. All the feelings, the difficult ones as well as the good ones, that I had for my father and mother went on God. The difficult ones such as the fear and the anger I had for both of my parents proved to be barriers to intimacy with God. I had to work them through in godly counseling and spiritual direction in order to gain closeness and trust, to develop a healthy dependence on God. The good ones, the love that was there, the respect I had particularly for Dad as a provider fueled and encouraged a connection with God.

I needed to take time to get to know this Christ, apart from the feelings I had for my earthly parents. I had to continually reach out to God to prove Him trustworthy enough to call Him Savior. It took time to kindle and rekindle the bond between us so that I could eventually rest in faith, trusting that He would supply my needs and be my all-in-all. This is so important for those prone to suicidal ideation.

Some can find some healing through other means, but it is only Christ who severs the spiritual encumbrances that hinder us at the deepest level. It is through a relationship with Christ that our heart-bond with fear and shame is severed as we seek forgiveness and love from Jesus. He comes in and unites our heart to God, the Holy Spirit, who resides inside of us when we surrender our heart to Christ. It is through Christ that we can experience comfort for the painful emotions associated with the past. In addition, there are layers of healing that take place throughout a lifetime. Even now, I am encountering Jesus' healing afresh in areas of deep insecurity.

I find I can be healed on one level, but I'm amazed to find that underneath still lies hidden pockets of pain, yet another layer of dysfunction that contributes to my difficulty in warding off temptations to self-harm. It is for these reasons that I still engage in personal godly counseling and in spiritual direction, as I've said, to maintain and promote spiritual health.

I've referred to myself as fear-hearted. I grew up fearing that I would get cancer and that strangers would enter our home. For years I had a habit of looking under the bed and in the closet before I could go to sleep, and in my teens, I felt the need to sterilize certain items, like the bathtub and the face cloth. I even used diluted ammonia as mouthwash for a while.

As a parent, you can only give what you know. My parents didn't know the God of love, so they could not be expected to lay a solid spiritual foundation on which I could build as an adult. If you, as a parent, are unwilling to explore the resources available to you through faith in Jesus Christ, you cannot be expected to raise your children with a true spiritual understanding that can help them stave off attacks from the enemy in later years, especially if he or she develops a suicidal predisposition.

As well, both of my parents had encountered emotional dysfunction in varying degrees in their families of origin; not having the opportunity to work this through, they inadvertently passed on at least some of their hurts to the next generation. This is why I have worked hard on accepting that life is difficult "at the core" by facing the deep hurts in me that come up from my childhood. Though I am not a parent, I seek to be as whole as I can so that I can relate healthily to others with appropriate boundaries. Certainly, a child who is raised in serious dysfunction by unhealthy parents can encounter abuse; whether the abuse is emotional, physical, or sexual, the child then can be more prone to develop a suicidal predisposition.

However, I reiterate, children need to be raised with the knowledge and an embracing of Ephesians 6:12 and of the two great commandments—to love God and love your neighbor as yourself.[1] If this does not happen, the child, in my opinion, is ill-equipped to face the spiritual warfare that he or she will encounter in adulthood. This is especially true if the child is not exposed to and taught about the power of prayer to Jesus and fasting.

As I've said, the fact is that we are all in a war, and when the heat is on, we may need to draw from childhood memories of our parents praying for us and with us, of our parents going to war for our souls and for our safety and physical well-being. We may need to draw on such as these to resist temptations to self-harm later in life.

Painful emotions of a mistreated child can become repressed. If he or she has no adequate outlet for them, as with a special aunt or other relative who befriends him or her, these difficult emotions can remain buried until the person decides to venture into the scary territory of the unconscious. These unresolved emotions can drain one of energy and can end up "running" the life of the person until he or she can take that leap of faith to get help.

One can find help through, perhaps, an older person, a mentor, or a counselor; consistent sharing and working through pain as it comes to the consciousness of the sufferer is paramount. For me, I found help in a therapeutic relationship, as I've spoken of earlier. It was by entering into therapy, as I started talking, little by little, more and more pain would surface to be healed.

Because I sought and eventually found a good therapist, I was able to come to the realization that my feelings mattered, were valid and real, that they were God-given. My mother was not in touch with her own feelings so could hardly have been expected to help train me to express mine.

In therapy, I was helped not only to see that my pain was understandable, but that I then had to take responsibility for it in order to find healing. I learned in therapy as well, how to interact with more social graces. With God's help, I am able to find strength and courage to enter into the process to face the damage that had been done ultimately by the evil one, a realization that has freed me from blaming my parents or any one person. This process has helped me gain strength to fend off thoughts of self-harm and given me a clearer view of my Savior; He reveals Himself to me and I come to know Him for who He is, as I work through painful feelings that were repressed in my childhood. Seeing Jesus in truth is key to living with and finding victory over a suicidal predisposition.

Suicidal Predisposition? Part 3

In a divorce where there are children involved, the little ones can be a constant reminder of the union between the couple that went sour. The children, in turn, can become inadvertent targets of rage and malice. Each member of the couple, in being with the children, can be reminded of the failure to keep the relationship going and thus become resentful and/or neglectful of the children. With one parent belittling and denigrating the other, not protecting the children from rage or even hatred toward each other, the child can become withdrawn, feeling as though to receive and give love to the "hated" parent is betraying the other one. Proper bonding with the parents can fail to take place for this child. This can contribute to the creation of a dependent personality.

Unmet dependency needs in childhood where the child is not allowed to foster a healthy dependence on his or her caregivers can leave that child clutching or clinging in desperation for support. In my case, I developed clingy, overly-trusting behavior, low self-esteem, inability to assert myself and a rabid hunger for connection. All this was I believe as a result of these unmet dependency needs.

With allowed and nourished dependence on the parents, the child can grow in security to eventually shift that dependence on them to dependence on God; this can lead to independence and then to healthy interdependence with others, which is what Jesus modeled in the garden of Gethsemane.[2] Both this dependence on God and learned interdependence are so crucial, as I've said, to a person's ability to cope well in adult years.

If the child is raised to develop a strong dependence on God, and this is modeled by his or her parents, spiritual maturity may develop over time, giving the person a stronger likelihood of staving off temptations to suicide in later years. I still have temptations, that is to say that I am still prone to suicidal tendencies, but I now have the understanding that it is not God who tempts. Suicide, I truly now believe, is the devil's work, as I've said.

To sum up, I have said what I have said in the past three parts on Suicidal Predisposition to say that there may be personalities that are more prone to becoming deeply suicidal in the wake of despair than others. Factors which may increase the likelihood of the development of a suicidal predisposition include the availability of a strong bond between the child and his or her parents or guardians fostering a healthy dependence in the child on his or her parents or guardians, exposure to mistreatment and serious dysfunction or abuse especially in the person's early years, the development of mental illness, to name a few. It is particularly people with these types of vulnerabilities who need special care and consideration not only from health care professionals but also from family and friends. Fundamentally though, those without a true spiritual understanding of the spiritual warfare in which we all find ourselves are in ultimate peril and are more prone to acting on suicidal ideation.

Other Risk Factors

Those who are highly sensitive and highly intelligent may also be at greater risk for suicide. Highly sensitive people can be more prone to take things personally, can pick up and be affected more deeply by the moods of others and therefore can become discouraged more easily.

Highly intelligent people may tend to think too much or not be able to rest in faith when answers don't come. They can get caught up in their mind and find it especially difficult to get down to a heart level. They may try to demand answers where only mystery lies, leading to despondency and despair.

"Above all else, guard your heart, for it is the well-spring of life."[3] This verse applies to all, but it strikes me that it is especially important for those who are highly sensitive and highly intelligent.

Chapter 16: "My Brother's Keeper"

After Cain had killed his brother Abel, God inquired about Abel's whereabouts. Cain replied, "I don't know. Am I my brother's keeper?"[1] If we ask that question in general, I would respond with a hearty yes. Let me explain.

We are all individuals responsible for ourselves, but we need each other; we need to operate in a web of interdependence, as I've said, depending on God as our head. I know I would have been helped if even one person, one teacher, one adult in my childhood and teenage years had sat me down and reached out to me, saying something like, "You seem troubled. What's on your mind?"

Being raised in an environment where I felt there was no one to reach to and no one reaching to me, to find a special someone who went out of his or her way to express concern could have been possibly life-changing. Certainly, if a professional or relative had taken me aside and asked me to describe the world I lived in when I was in my delusional state, perhaps the paralysis could have been averted.

We need to reach out to those around us who are hurting, as God leads. We need to reach out in an non-intrusive, loving way so that the hurting person can get the message that someone cares, that that person feels that they matter, that the person does not feel that they are invisible and being left into someone else's hands.

Preacher Edward Victor Hill, who fed and clothed the homeless in Los Angeles, said that we are "it"—that God has chosen no one and nothing else to spread his love and truth. We're it! You're it! You are Jesus' hands, feet, eyes, mouth, etc.! Jesus is living His life here on earth through you! Take seriously your role as a conduit of Christ's love. You have more of a role to play than you think.

Just remember that you will be held accountable for how you used your gifts and abilities, whether you spread His love or not. Recall Jesus' words, "By this all men will know that you are my disciples, if you love one another."[2] Sharing love should be your trademark as a Christian. We are, after all, ambassadors, representatives of Christ Himself. You may be the closest thing to Christ that some people ever meet.

Especially family members of a person with a tendency toward suicidal ideation need to tread very carefully, taking seriously their relative in pain. Friends as well, do not be afraid to enter into the world of the ill person. Do not ignore him/her or hope that the person's illness will go away on its own. The one who is prone to suicidal ideation is in need of sensitive, caring individuals to come alongside.

I remember telling someone I had jumped off a bridge and her response was of disbelief because she felt that life was "so sweet." Those who have not experienced the relentless nature of ongoing suicidal ideation may find it hard to relate to someone who has considered or is contemplating or has attempted suicide.

All the more reason that we are our brother's keeper, not only our suicidal brother or sister, but those who we know are down or discouraged. I say again, we need to take seriously our roles as conduits of Christ. We need to stick by and especially close to those in great pain, whether it be emotional, physical, or spiritual, because it is these folks who are especially vulnerable to the attacks of the enemy. Jesus referred to folk such as these as the "least of these,"[3] ones in whom Christ's presence can be especially strong. Get involved: his or her very life, certainly his or her quality of life may depend on your help, advocacy, and/or intervention, and you may get truly blessed because you did.

Indifference

We often are not our brother's keeper because of this disease known as indifference. It has been said that this is the opposite of love, not hate, as one may at first assume. Indifference denies the interconnectedness—the need for interdependence—within humanity. In my childhood, I walked around in a cloud of despair and confusion; it was evident in many of the pictures taken at that time. Yet so many turned their eyes from the elephant in the room. Some even fed him and took care of him, all the while stepping carefully around the bleeding soul that was me.

When I grew up, I discovered a whole world that did just that, including the psychiatric system. I reiterate: had there been a proactive teacher or relative or professional in my life at various points, who saw to it that I got the help I so obviously needed, who knows where I would be today? And who knows where you would be today if not for this disease called indifference.

In Ruin

Sometimes because of indifference but sometimes because God allows or chooses not to intervene, our lives can come to ruin. "(T)his is what the Sovereign LORD says: ... 'A ruin! A ruin! I will make it a ruin!'"[4] Perhaps you find that this describes your life right now.

Shortly after arriving at the institution, about a year post-injury, I wrote these words: "I feel like I am in ruin in virtually every way. Sexually, I have no feeling below. Emotionally, I struggle with depression on a daily basis. Socially, it's so difficult to make new friends from this barrier called a wheelchair. Physically, I have frequent bladder infections and regular pain in my legs. Recreationally, I can no longer swim like I used to or walk. Spiritually, I can no longer get out in the heart of creation like I used to, and I have to listen to all kinds of noise throughout the day and night. Financially, I get $112 a month on which to live."

About three years later, I wrote: "I am so blessed. I have use of my hands and my mind. I have dear family and friends who love me and show me regularly. I have a place I can call home that is quiet and private. I have been blessed with some of God's richest blessings: joy, peace, faith, hope, love, strength, courage. I can give love and receive it, because God is love, and He has filled me with Himself. Freely I have been given, so freely I will give."

I had gone from abject hatred and disdain for life to free-flowing love, joy, and peace with Christ and His body. When I lived in the institution, I had been encouraged to return to the church I was in before the jump. I credit this transformation to Christ, of course, but also to my church, the body of believers, where I found love and acceptance. I truly believe that it is in community that we find victory, as I've said.

There is a song sung by Jill Phillips that says, "Triumph and tragedy, only God can be both the builder and the wrecking ball." Certainly, in our finite understanding, we can see Him as one or the other. However, clearly God says in His Word, "For my thoughts are not your thoughts, neither are your ways my ways,' declares the LORD."[5] This is personally my favorite verse of Scripture. What you see as ruinous, God may view in another way.

By the world's standards, Jesus' life on earth came to ruin; He was brutally beaten and left to die on a Roman cross aside two thieves. And it was the Father's will for His Beloved Son. But, as we look with spiritual eyes, oh, what spiritual riches, your eternal salvation and mine was won on that cross—from that situation that was by all worldly standards ruinous. If you feel that all about you is ruin, watch, wait, trust, and see what God can do.

Another Dawn at the Institution

Four months after admission to the institution, still feeling like my life was in ruin, I wrote this:

"The dawn comes mercilessly in the institution. I am bothered once again by bright lights overhead and noisy voices in the hall. I love the night even though I lie awake for hours in my own perspiration. A kidney infection has wreaked havoc in my body. Nausea steeps into my pores.

Yet I love the night–the only time of some consistent quiet. I think of my friend who spent twenty-nine years in this institution. He is without the use of his hands, arms, or legs. He got out to live in an apartment.

A patient is agitated now. Exceedingly agitated. Chattering loudly, babbling really. Making no sense. Breaks in the silence. Now the nurses come to attend to my neighbor. Talking without restraint at 6 a.m. Raising their voices at the patient. 'Didn't I tell you not to do that?' and 'Turn!' they command vigorously. One looks at me writing and walks away.

Balbina, my neighbor, complains of feeling 'hot like a fever;' they say nothing. One nurse ventures to ask if I'm okay, a stroke of kindness. I look at the time. It is fixed on 6:12 a.m., seeming as though it could stay there, or maybe I want it to. But lo and behold, mercilessly it cranks on.

It is now 6:14. Time watched seems to go slowly and is deceivingly slow, because I go from these relatively quiet moments to the passing of weeks. I notice now I'm feeling tired. The malaise is still there. Better try to rest before the night is over completely and the din returns with another dawn at the institution."

Chapter 17: Suffering Quietly

God calls us to share in Jesus' sufferings, and I really believe that He is looking for people to do it quietly– quietly, not silently. Tell your story, tell it when and with whomever you trust, but don't do it with an angry or complaining spirit. By whomever, I mean counselors, friends, relatives, anyone you can trust. Let people know.

People need to hear about your suffering so they know more how to pray, and so they can get a before and after picture. God can bless people who can articulate what they are going through, by teaching others from it, inspiring them and giving them a glimpse of God at work. Share your suffering, but do it quietly.

On Bullies

Maybe there is someone or some people in your life who are bullies. Some of the suffering I experienced while in the institution took the form of "superiors" or "nurses" who were bullies. (I refer you here to the poem, *Sour*.)

I didn't take it personally. I understood that they just demonstrated their own insecurity by trying to control through anger and hurt. I knew that they did not cope well with their own vulnerability.

I processed the mistreatment by dealing with the anger I had for situations that would arise with a friend or in a counseling session. It actually helped me to cope by writing the incidents down and reporting them when they happened to the nurse manager. Though the complaints procedure in the institution was generally circular, and little to nothing ultimately came of my complaint, I still felt that by doing this, I would take a stand for justice. I recognized that many of these "superiors" had a need to control through hurting others out of their own deep-seated fears, and yet, it was something against which I felt I needed to take a stand.

Perhaps they were bullied in some way in their lives, particularly in their childhoods, and they had learned to approach the vulnerable by squashing their spirits, as they perhaps had done to them. Unfortunately, they have had not grown from their experience but have carried on the cycle of abuse.

Seeing abusers this way helped me to cope. Perhaps it can help you. I would not only report incidents of abuse and the perpetrators, but I would also pray for them. After all, we are called to "love our enemies and pray for those who persecute (us)."[1] This would free me to "love the sinner but hate the sin." It gave me the ability to separate the two.

Enduring the suffering in this way gave me not only self-control, which is a fruit of the Spirit[2], but a deepened, richer relationship to Jesus as I relied on Him for strength and took a stand for what I felt was His justice. Still, the suffering in the institution, at times, was relentless. It caused me sometimes to say: "Haven't I suffered enough?"

Haven't I Suffered Enough?

Before I accepted at a deeper level that life is difficult, I wanted/expected things to go my way, and when they didn't, I was disappointed. Somehow I had in the back of my mind that I'd suffered enough, and I deserved for things to go well. I thought that somehow since I'd suffered for God and endured, I should have been earning favor with God. I believed that He ought to, therefore, be lenient with me.

But, suffering is no respecter of persons; even it seems that God heaps it on those He loves, as a way to make us more like Him. Joni Eareckson Tada, author, speaker, radio host, and quadriplegic, says that Jesus puts suffering between you and He so that there will be nothing between you and He.

Certainly, Paul suffered greatly (see 2 Cor. 11:23–28 to find him boasting in his sufferings). Paul wrote some of the greatest words ever penned because he endured. Indeed, Jesus had to suffer willingly and in the most excruciating way for us to have the Savior of the world.

Someone once said that we do not come to God because things are going so well that we want someone to thank. It is through suffering that He draws us to Himself. When I was in the throws of depression over having given up my daughter for adoption in late 1986,

God wooed me. It was in the summer of 1987 that so many monarch butterflies came in my line of vision that I started to think that Someone was trying to get my attention. That's how I came to believe in God.

Shortly thereafter, knowing nothing of the butterflies, a friend invited me to her church, where I accepted Christ into my heart on an altar call. God used creation, an obedient pastor, and that suffering to draw me to Himself and seal my eternal destiny for all time, but that was only the beginning of the work He planned to do in me.

God has a plan for you too. He will take your suffering and use it for His purposes if you can trust Him with it. You may never, while you are on this earth, get the answers that you hope for regarding God's eternal reasons for allowing your suffering. That's where faith comes in; He asks us only to trust Him in it. Take your frustrations, your questions about your suffering to Him. He may not reveal the answers, as I've said, but one day, we will know all. Please be patient and wait for that day; wait for His time. It will come faster than you think.

Freedom through Paralysis

I truly believe there is freedom through deep suffering like mine and like yours. (I refer you here to my poem called, *Freedom*.)

I went sailing with a volunteer. In speaking with him, being on the open water, I found myself saying that I've found enormous freedom because of my injury. I acquired a freedom from things, things that really don't matter much in the long run. I acquired a freedom from idolatry, including idolatry of my home. I remember seeing on the TV homes going up in flames; I thought to myself after being thrust from my residence that even homes are expendable—that we ought not to put our faith in them, but in Christ alone.

Jesus says to the rich young man, "Go, sell everything you have and give to the poor, and you will have treasure in heaven. Then come, follow me."[3] Jesus taught me not to put my value into temporal, earthly things because I can't take them with me. Only that which is honed in my character through suffering, for example, only Christ-likeness, is of eternal value.

Now I'm much more appreciative of things I used to previously take for granted. I now thank God for a roof over my head. I thank God for food in my stomach. I thank God for the abilities I do have: the use of my hands and arms, my sight, my hearing, my voice. In the institution, I met people like Paul Capon, who uses a device with a keyboard in order to "talk." I try to think of everything as a blessing from God. I thank Him for the relatives and friends who struggle to love and relate to me. I thank Him for the sunshine, for pretty flowers that delight, for all of creation.

I value my relationship to Christ above all, including the heart-to-heart conversations I have with Him. I value these with people as well. I value what I call love moments—moments of tenderness between me and my caregivers, me and my loved ones. God has really revealed to me where to put my energy and has pointed me in directions to speak about Him, to be His minister, in ways I would have missed or felt inadequate to address prior to the injury.

Certainly, I see woundedness, I see Jesus everywhere I go—in the bus driver, in the elderly, in the disabled, in the able-bodied. I see vulnerability and fragility, and I want to help bring spiritual renewal and fortification in the form of Jesus Christ. I reach out to help offer Christ where it's appropriate, who is the source of my help, my joy, and my spiritual freedom.

Because of the wheelchair, I found myself saying words of comfort, for instance, to a fellow traveler in a wheelchair, with this person sensing that "my Christ" could actually reach him/her in the space where he/she is, and could even bring, not only comfort, but salvation. "To the weak, I became weak, to win the weak"[4], said Paul. Just trust that Jesus is doing something beautiful spiritually in and through your deep suffering. "The truth will set you free"[5]: embrace the truth about your painful situation and you, too, will find freedom.

Chapter 18: Pleasure in Illness

I tended to relish the attention I was given when I was ill. I remember as a teenager being in "heaven" when I had mononucleosis. My mother was more apt to be kind to me at that time. It was a chance to receive some real care. It was a chance to become the center of attention. Perhaps you can relate to this. For those who experienced loving behaviors and attitudes from parents more so when you were ill as children, there can be a form of "pleasure" taken in being ill.

In contrast, know that your loving Heavenly Father loves you no matter what the circumstances, though I personally have found that when I am ill, I tend to think more about Him. I draw near to Him and I feel Him drawing near to me. If you find yourself in a serious illness, draw near to Him. He is calling you to this through the pain. He wants to love you in a special, eternal way.

Perhaps you find that you cannot make sense of your suffering and why God is allowing it, especially if your condition is deteriorating. (I refer you here to my poem, *Eternal Love*.) Trust that there is a purpose: even those barely alive can draw compassion and gratitude out of the one who interacts with him or her. When we see someone who is very debilitated, we can feel sadness or compassion, which can draw us to the ill one in community and to God. Just as my illness as a teenager drew kindness out of my mother, it can have the same effect on others witnessing you in your pain. If you feel alone in your pain, let me assure you that with Christ you are not alone. Someone once said that, when Christ is all you have, you realize He is all you need. Truly, reach out to and lean on Him who knows all and can do anything. Remember, "with God, all things are possible."[1]

I believe there is a spiritual richness to those who are very incapacitated, that there is great meaning and purpose in the suffering. God draws near to such as these and has special insight and blessings to shower not only on them but on those who love them.

Know that He has eternal reasons for doing the things He does. Rest in faith, knowing that He has things in His control, that He is working out His purposes in and through you as you submit and surrender your suffering to Him. He wants to use this time to show you how very special you are and to fill you and others with His Spirit. It's not so wrong if you experience some "pleasure" in your illness because of the attention you receive, just keep reaching out and looking up. You will find not only the horizontal but divine, vertical attention from Jesus, the Great Physician.

Take Up Your Cross

As we take up our cross, we can look to the vertical, to Christ, as well as to Scripture. The Bible is created for people to keep on, to endure. It's one big encouragement book. The purpose it was written is to advise and to guide as to how to proceed, not to recede. Jesus said, "If anyone would come after me, he must deny himself and take up his cross and follow me."[2] Jesus uses the word "must," not "may."

If you feel like giving up, know that suicide is not a denying self; it is an indulging self. For me, it was the ultimate act of hedonism. I believed I would go to a pain-free, blissful existence alongside my Savior. It was about pride and feelings. It is a way of saying to God, "I know best and I feel I really want to do this." It is not following Jesus' example when He said, "(N)ot as I will, but as you will."[3]

Luke reports that Jesus said, "If anyone would come after me, he must deny himself and take up his cross daily and follow me."[4] Satan has a version of this: "If anyone would come after me, he must indulge himself to *feel* better right now and lay down his cross and follow me."

It is indeed in taking one day at a time, seeking the Spirit so that we can find strength to wrestle with difficult feelings one at a time, but keeping our eyes fixed on Jesus, not on the feelings that we can find victory. Jesus Himself said it best, "(D)o not worry about tomorrow, for tomorrow will worry about itself. Each day has enough trouble of its own."[5]

If I have learned anything from my suicide attempt, it's that life is not about feelings, as I've said. Feelings come and go; life is filled with ups and downs. Feelings change, hurts heal, resilient spirits adjust to circumstances. Certainly I found that I even adjusted to living in the institution. Though I had no consistent quiet or privacy, I still found I had good days, as well as bad days, when I was there. It's on these bad days that I had to cling with that much more desperation to Jesus for strength and comfort to see me through until they pass. Don't act out on a bad day. Instead, take up your cross and walk with Christ, a minute at a time if necessary.

Do not be afraid to acknowledge your deep need for help, your fragility, your vulnerability. Paul said, "If I must boast, I will boast of the things that show my weakness."[6] Paul was given a thorn in his flesh[7]; he pleaded three times for God to remove it. Jesus simply said to Paul, "My grace is sufficient for you, for my power is made perfect in weakness."[8] Jesus is drawing near to you in your pain. Won't you extend your hand to Him? Certainly, I reiterate that we are all helpless, whether able-bodied or not, before Jesus. The reality of tsunamis, earthquakes, and hurricanes attest to this. Why not acknowledge this, and as you take up your cross, look to omnipotence for help?

Down times will come when we will feel that fragility, that vulnerability more intensely. It is especially in these times that we need to cling to the Savior, as I've said, and to Scriptural truth—such promises of God as this: "Being confident of this, that he who began a good work in you will carry it on to completion until the day of Christ Jesus."[9] Remember this if you are standing on your bridge about to lay down your cross.

Paul on Departing

Paul knew the temptation of laying down his cross. He writes:

> For to me, to live is Christ and to die is gain. If I am to go on living in the body, this will mean fruitful labor for me. Yet what shall I choose? I do not know! I am torn between the two: I desire to depart and be with Christ, which is better by far; but it is more necessary for you that I remain in the body.
>
> Convinced of this, I know that I will remain, and I will continue with all of you for your progress and joy in the faith, so that through my being with you again your joy in Christ Jesus will overflow on account of me. [10]

Paul knew what it was to want to be with Jesus. He knew deep suffering (see 2 Corinthians 11:16–29 where Paul boasts in his sufferings). And he comes to the conclusion that he needed to remain on the earth. He understood as well that people would be hurt and grieved if he were to depart and perhaps take his death into his own hands. Others gain inspiration and hope and, as Paul writes here, "joy" in seeing him press on. Your moving forward can have the same effect on others around you.

Treasures in Heaven

In moving forward, we can build up treasures. Jesus says,

> Do not store up for yourselves treasures on earth,
> where moth and rust destroy and where thieves
> break in and steal. But store up for yourselves
> treasures in heaven, where moth and rust do
> not destroy, and where thieves do not break in
> and steal. For where your treasure is, there your
> heart will be also.[11]

Each day we have the opportunity to gather more treasures in heaven to enjoy for all eternity. Each day that we forge on, there are new opportunities to share Christ, to encourage someone, to build someone up, to offer some hope, to store up more goodies, that when our time comes to pass from this earth, we will enjoy our rewards for all eternity. "Serve wholeheartedly, as if you were serving the LORD, not men, because you know that the LORD will reward everyone for whatever good he does, whether he is slave or free."[12] It's all built a day, sometimes an hour or a minute at a time, as I've said.

Chapter 19: Vicarious Enjoyment

I am able to watch people and gain vicarious enjoyment. When I was at the Canadian National Exhibition, for example, I would like to watch the people on the rides.

To watch the folk go up and down, to see the smiles and laughter, would thrill me. I would also like to watch riders on horses there since that was one of my favorite pastimes. I like to watch people do all sorts of things, including walking, running, playing with their children. I derive pleasure from and now take time to observe simple things that I used to take for granted. Perhaps you too, who are confined in some way, can find some pleasure vicariously.

Entering In

I not only derive pleasure vicariously, but by entering in to the lives of those around me. By entering in to the lives of those around me in a polite, friendly way, I have found that I can gain fulfillment and satisfaction. I try to enter in as much as is possible. Where appropriate, I talk to those around me about what they experience, what their reality is. Whoever they are, co-workers, nurses, doctors, children, superiors, I try to non-intrusively enter in. I speak to them about the weather, ask them about their day, how they are, etc. I try to meet them where they are at. Some people will not let you in; they put up barriers and/or answer tersely. Others will engage with you, making that connection.

Attendants come into my home and help me with tasks that I cannot manage on my own. There are those who interact with me in a holistic way, and those who merely do the physical task and leave. Some see me as a whole person and others see me as a disability. I notice that those in the former group seem to more often come and go with a smile on their face, whereas from those in the latter group, I feel their sense of tedium and drudgery.

A Sadder Place

When life becomes tedium and drudgery, we can long for home. I understand how strongly Satan can push a person into believing that he or she wants to die. It can feel like a need, as much as we have for food or for water, as I've said. That's why a suicidal person needs to be protected, needs to be put into hospital, or to be around supportive, understanding people during the period when he or she feels that way.

I understand if you presently feel or have felt that you want to die. And I'm here to say to you that it would be a sadder place without you. There would be an empty space where you were, a lonely empty space where your warm, beating-heart body was—for all eternity. You would be missed; the contribution you are intended to make in this world would forever be lost. It would be a sadder place without you. Forever.

Mud or Stars?

A change in perspective can be so helpful when one is suicidal. I quote again from Dr. M. Scott Peck: "life is difficult." Life takes perseverance. Life needs hope. Life requires patience. And when we're spent and in despair, life can lead us to thoughts of death. As life corners us in, we may be left to ponder suicide. There will be days like that, especially for most of us with mental illness, as suicidal ideation can be a symptom.

Thoughts of death can become an obsession, an addiction, and feel as strong as a need, as I've mentioned. I used to enjoy walking in cemeteries. In cemeteries is where I would feel most at home. I dwelt on thoughts of death, even to receive comfort. These thoughts provided me with an escape from a world I felt was harsh, cold, and cruel.

I was depressed as a child. I knew depression. I lived, spent much time in the black. I experienced my world not as a loving, protected place, but a hostile place in which I felt I did not belong. Thoughts of suicide encouraged my depression and were almost like comfort food for the mind to me. I was at home in the depths. Thoughts of suicide became like the "candy of despair." Depression was such familiar territory that I would allow myself to revel in thoughts of suicide like I was enjoying a hard candy.

A dwelling on thoughts of suicide, however, is entertaining the devil. He can use it to exhaust and reinforce hopelessness. Now I believe that those thoughts originate from the pit of hell. I need to dismiss them and lay them aside when they come now. Indeed, dwelling on these thoughts is a leaning into Satan.

I was able to overcome my tendency to dwell on suicidal ideation by offering everything and anything up in prayer. Suicidal ideation is a looking down, actually a staring down, whereas prayer is a looking up. If you are despairing, can you get your gaze off your circumstances, out of the black, and look into the eyes of the Savior? Can you lay your heart bare before Him as He made Himself so vulnerable for you by allowing Himself to be beaten, mocked, ridiculed, and crucified on a cruel Roman cross? If you are finding your reality cruel, can you remember what He suffered for you?

I found great comfort in pouring out my heart to Jesus, and, in turn, listening to his reply. Truly that dialogue is what life is worth living for, for me. Oscar Wilde once said, "Two men looked through prison bars. One saw mud, the other stars." Looking down comes naturally for those who are used to it. You need to train yourself to tread into, perhaps, new territory and persevere with looking up into His loving eyes. Remember, you cannot see both stars and mud at the same time. You see either one or the other.

Chapter 20: Disabled

I see people everywhere who are staring into the mud. I see disabled people all around me: people who walk but suffer from paralysis of the will. (See my poem, *Paralysis of the Will*.) These people live in a state of low-grade depression; they are living what Charles Stanley calls a "settle-for life," going wearily from one day to the next, not willing to resolve the deep issues that weigh them down and often not even realizing or recognizing the problem. They are trying so hard in self-effort that they are exhausted.

Some are blinded by denial and are too strong to be weak. It takes courage to allow oneself to be vulnerable, to acknowledge one's own brokenness, to give up dependence on self and realize the need for dependence on God.

This wheelchair, though it has made me more in need of people even for basic activities like showers, has liberated me to lean more heavily on God. Dependence on God is always good, for God is 100% trustworthy, unlike any human being. When I was newly injured, I cursed God and would not have used the adjective "trustworthy" to describe Him. He has, however, in true Romans 8:28

fashion, slowly turned my paralysis around, used it for His glory, and forged a deeper and much more profound eternity for me than if I had not been injured.

God is ultimately the provider of all our needs; I see my caregivers as merely an extension of God's hand at work. I may be physically disabled, but through utter dependence on God, I am free in my spirit and in my will. After all, I reiterate that it is in the spirit that we soar. If you think you may be paralyzed by fear in your will, trust Him today and watch as slowly, little by little, He moves you forward.

Pleasure versus Joy

When we soar, we can feel immense joy. It strikes me that there is a difference between pleasure and joy. Some it seems opt for seeking sensual pleasures, like those involved in premarital sex or fornication, for instance. "Now to the unmarried and the widow I say: It is good for them to stay unmarried, as I am. But if they cannot control themselves, they should marry, for it is better to marry than to burn with passion,"[1] (see also 1 Corinthians 6:13–16, 7:3–5). Recall also, "Put to death, therefore, whatever belongs to your earthly nature: sexual immorality, impurity, lust, evil desires, and greed, which is idolatry."[2] To me, those involved in this type of sin have exchanged pleasure for the joy that God places in our hearts as a result of our obedience.

Consider these two passages: Paul says,

So I say, live by the Spirit, and you will not gratify

the desires of the sinful nature. For the sinful nature desires what is contrary to the Spirit, and the Spirit what is contrary to the sinful nature. They are in conflict with each other, so that you do not do what you want.[3]

Paul also states,

> I do not understand what I do. For what I want to do I do not do, but what I hate I do. And if I do what I do not want to do, I agree that the law is good. As it is, it is no longer I myself who do it, but it is sin living in me. I know that nothing good lives in me, that is, in my sinful nature. For I have the desire to do what is good, but I cannot carry it out. For what I do is not the good I want to do; no, the evil I do not want to do—this I keep on doing.[4]

In light of these last two passages in particular, be gentle with yourself if you find yourself indulging the sinful nature, realizing that you are in a war. Remember that "our struggle is against the spiritual forces of evil," as laid out in Ephesians 6:10–12. We are not perfect; only Jesus is sinless. We are prone to falling.

Recall Jesus' teaching regarding the woman caught in adultery whom the teachers of the Law and the Pharisees wanted to stone. "'If any one of you is without sin, let him be the first to throw a stone at her.' ... At this, those who heard began to go away one at a time, the older ones first, until only Jesus was left, with the woman still standing there."[5] Recall as well that Jesus forgave her: "(N)either do I condemn you ... Go now and leave your life of sin."[6]

Can we receive, as this woman did, Jesus' tenderness and forgiveness when we fall?

Getting back to Paul, he describes the "fruit of the Spirit," which is "love, joy, peace, patience, kindness, goodness, faithfulness, gentleness, and self-control."[7] God actually builds these qualities into the life of a Christian who walks by the Spirit, not indulging self in ungodly pleasures but finding strength in the joy of the LORD. Unbelievers can try to display these fruits through self-effort, but it is actually God in the devoted Christian's life who produces these qualities as an offshoot of obedience as he or she, faithfully walking in step with the Spirit, surrenders self-will and self-government and gives up control of his or her life to God.

For friends or relatives of yours or maybe for yourself who believe that life is good without God, let me tell you that living in the power of the Holy Spirit is better than any ecstasy the world has to offer. To feel God interacting with me through song, written, or spoken word, through people, to actually sense the supernatural is life at its finest. That is how I can be referred to as "Ellen of Joy" yet within a metal frame.

Whatever benefits or earthly pleasures a person may be reaping by indulging the sinful or earthly nature, the opportunity to have the fruit of the Spirit in one's life is well worth the "sacrifice" one may feel one makes to give up worldly ways.

> He (Moses) chose to be mistreated along with the people of God rather than to enjoy the pleasures of sin for a short time. He regarded disgrace for the sake of Christ as of greater

value than the treasures of Egypt, because he was looking ahead to his reward. [8]

Can we, like Moses, choose to set aside the fleeting pleasures of sin so we can have the reward of joy in obedience for now and in eternity?

God fills me with joy, among other rich fruit, when I seek Him and follow Him. I suggest to you that if you, as a Christian, have given in to ungodly pleasures, you are indeed forfeiting true joy, for this fruit cannot grow from the seed of sin. Receive Jesus' tender forgiveness through genuine repentance, using this as a model to then forgive yourself.

Chapter 21: Ellen's Recipe for Life

Heavy daily doses of Scripture

Deep and courageous, daily, heart-to-heart dialogue with God in prayer and in fellowship with others

Regular but non-intrusive entering-in to the lives of those around you

Disciplined walks of thirty minutes daily or near daily

Disciplined work, preferably in an area that uses your gifts

Scriptural meditations weekly: I use the "Lectio Divina" method, which involves silence and journaling and is followed by spiritual direction.

Scriptural Meditations: How to Pray with Scripture

Throughout Scripture,[1] we are encouraged to ponder God's Word, to listen, and to meditate. In listening prayer, there are no failures. Just being open to God, letting go of expectations, God speaks. He can also give a real sense of quietness and peace through the process.

Listening Prayer or "Lectio Divina" involves reading a passage a few times slowly. If the passage is a narrative (such as John 13:1–17, where Jesus washes His disciples' feet), you are invited to put yourself in the story, using your imagination, becoming one of the people, and using all five senses so the scene becomes alive and unfolds. You can respond to the other people in the passage and the situation through journaling. (This process is also known as Ignatian Contemplation.)

If the passage is non-narrative (such as a Psalm or part thereof), you can stay with the word, phrase, or whole verse that "lights up" for you. God is speaking through this. You are encouraged to soak in the words or images or repeat them gently to "digest" them, like a cow chewing her cud. Then you can dialogue with Jesus over the thoughts and feelings that came to you, responding to God from your heart. You can here just be still and enjoy God's presence in silence, exchanging love. Following a period of silence, you can again journal what comes to you after re-reading the passage once again.

Spiritual direction is an interpersonal interaction in which the spiritual director assists a person to growth in the Spirit, strengthening faith, giving hope in terms of difficulties, sufferings, and trials, and promoting love, for instance, in the person's life within the context of the Christian community. It involves clarification and discernment of God's voice in the life of the individual.

My Selfish Need

Personally, I have a selfish need. Perhaps you have been considering or have in the past contemplated suicide. Forgive me, but I have a selfish need to have you around. I know you may feel Satan's relentless attacks through regular suicidal ideation. There were times when the enemy filled my mind, when thoughts of ending it engulfed me. I was, in fact, driven by thoughts of harming myself. Day after day I would fantasize about an end to the pain, a blissful release into the arms of Jesus.

In the garden of Gethsemane, Jesus said, "My Father, if it is possible, may this cup be taken from me. Yet not as I will, but as you will."[2] If the Father had intended Jesus to die then, certainly the Father could have accomplished that. He had a purpose in the suffering of Jesus, in the beatings, the mockings, and in the cross that are His and His alone. The Father chose to fulfill His purpose through suffering. So it is with your suffering. He is fulfilling His purpose for you through your suffering, something He may only reveal to you when you meet Him on your Judgment Day. You need to try and trust, to have faith. I know relentless agony, I assure you. Just try to hang on even one hour at a time. I encourage you as I do for myself.

I know how selfish I can be at my core, that I want you to go on despite your great suffering for me and my well-being. I want to have you around. I want you to go on so I do not have to feel the feelings that will come if you go before your (His) time: the guilt, the anger, the sorrow. I would like to have you continue for my sake. I need another human role model other than Jesus of how someone in intense suffering endures.

A song says, "I'm tired of living but I'm afraid to die." If you too feel this way, you need to get connected, to get plugged in to the power source, Jesus Christ, in a big way to help you overcome that fatigue. You can do this by regular Bible-reading, desperate and sincere prayer, attending a Bible-believing church regularly, sharing your heart honestly with others who care, and above all, obeying Jesus as you let Him lead you. He would never command you to destroy yourself. That desire, that temptation does not come from God. Jesus says, "The thief comes only to steal and kill and destroy; I have come that they may have life, and have it to the full."[3] Spiritual warfare is a reality; please take it seriously.

James says, "(E)ach one is tempted when, by his own evil desire, he is dragged away and enticed."[4] Satan can influence the heart that is "deceitful above all things"[5] by gaining entry into your mind with suicidal thoughts so that there is no room for any other thoughts. He will try to use the feelings of despair and the natural wickedness of the human heart to overwhelm and engulf you.

Imagine how many lost their lives in natural disasters who were not ready to die. Imagine the folk who were diagnosed with a terminal illness when life was previously good. Imagine all those who succeeded in taking their lives, only to feel deep regret when they got to the other side. Imagine all those who attempted suicide and survived, and later told of how glad they were that they did not succeed. He knows all about what you're suffering. He knows more about you than you know about yourself. Won't you hand your pain over to Him, who is bigger than your problems?

God has gifted you with your various abilities. Reach into yourself and imagine what life would be like without them. Do the work of entering into the world of the disabled. It will give you a greater appreciation for your own life. You may be surprised to meet Jesus there. He can change your despair to rivers of gratitude and thankfulness. "He has sent me ... to bestow on them a crown of beauty instead of ashes, the oil of gladness instead of mourning, and a garment of praise instead of a spirit of despair."[6] (The "me" in this verse may refer to Isaiah in a limited sense, but the Messianic servant is the main figure intended here. Jesus, in fact, applied Isaiah 61:1–2 to himself in Luke 4:16–21 and Matthew 11:5.)

Remember my favorite verse: " 'My ways are not your ways, neither are my thoughts your thoughts,' declares the LORD."[7] What you are suffering may be incomprehensible to you. Here I amplify Proverbs 3:5–6:

> Trust in the LORD with all your heart and lean not on your own (finite, human) understanding (to comprehend the eternal God); in all (not "some" of) your ways acknowledge him, and he will make your paths straight (not crooked and haphazard).

It doesn't say that He will explain everything. You have to be patient for Judgment Day for that, as I've said.

We do need to be patient and enduring. You have a resilient spirit, more resilient than you know. Often the most difficult time is the onset of the painful experience.

I was intensely suicidal just after my injury, but slowly, over years, I came to the understanding I now have that I am not my own but am God's possession, that suicide is indeed a sin. Through patient endurance, your spirit too can adjust. Glean from Jesus' strength when you are facing your Gethsemane. Look also to Job.

What if Job would have committed suicide? He would not have been able to enjoy the blessings that God bestowed on him after his time of suffering was over, and even more importantly, Job would not have come to the understanding nor had the insights into God that he had if he had not endured his suffering. Job said, after speaking to his "comforters" and to the LORD Himself, "Surely I spoke of things I did not understand, things too wonderful for me to know ... My ears had heard of you but now my eyes have seen you. Therefore I despise myself and repent in dust and ashes."[8] It seems Job had regret for speaking as he had about and to God. Certainly I had regret for cursing God when I was newly injured, breaking the first and greatest commandment to "(l)ove God with your heart and with all your soul and with all your mind"[9] and for saying I would never forgive Him.

I reiterate: I have a need, a selfish need to have you around. I do not want to go through the pain, the grief that I would feel if you left this earth. And I need to learn from you about what it is to go through what you're going through. I need a model, an earthly example of what it is to suffer and to succeed in and through it. I need a model of another person with a strong faith who trusts in God in the most difficult of circumstances.

Remember, you are being watched, especially by those who love you. You will not know just how many people you will impact with your patient endurance until you face Jesus on your Judgment Day. Cling to Him who is the answer, and let those around you learn what it is to endure through faith. What a testimony you can be to Jesus' triumphant spirit in you!

Chapter 22: Relentless Agony—Grief Expressed

Secretly I wished everyone would suffer a spinal cord injury so I did not have to feel so alone. Secretly hoping to counsel one day but seeing myself so moody, so messed up, feeling so forlorn, that I figure I'll never be any earthly good. Because it's raining and raining and raining. The clouds part for a brief moment and a little sun peaks out, but then it clouds over again and it rains and rains and rains. Relentless agony.

I wrote this while living in the institution. Two years later, as I've said, I was referred to as "Ellen of Joy." I began to counsel again too. He can take your pain and use it: the period of time you spend in relentless agony translates into courage for the onlooker who watches you go through your trial. And this period will pass. Keep on keeping on, won't you please?

Shame

I encourage you to keep on, because no matter what anyone says, there is a shame associated with suicide. No matter what the circumstances, no matter what the situation, there is a black mark against the one who commits suicide as well as against the family. No one ever commends the one who attempts suicide for his or her courage. It does take courage to attempt suicide; it takes more sometimes to go on.

After I jumped and was in rehab, I felt a cloud of shame following me. People would ask me how I got into the wheelchair, and I would be flooded with shame. Now I have come to see that I was not to blame, because my mind was not in my control. Nonetheless, my story carries with it a blackness that is contained specifically in the suicide attempt. Certainly there is no pride in what I did, there is no sense of victory. The victory and the pride come as I face the consequences and go on now in a paralyzed state.

If you feel you have done something terribly wrong and feel shame, go to Jesus. Ask for His forgiveness and receive it. When I repented of my suicide attempt, I felt God give me such relief and such gratitude at being alive, as I've mentioned. There is healing for shame. Seek it and then brush yourself off. It takes courage to get up and stand and begin walking again after a serious fall.

Remorse

Not only shame, but the jump carried with it a tremen-

dous sense of remorse and regret. I felt a profound sadness, a deep remorse that I could not love myself enough
to have resisted the temptation to try to end my life, and
deep sadness for the pain I caused those who love me,
indeed, for myself as well. God, however, has melted
regret away as I have had the privilege of watching Him
work all things for good in true Romans 8:28 fashion.

I thank God that I have a chance now to warn and tell
others about suicide. Perhaps that is part of the reason
why God allowed the paralysis in my life—to speak into
your life. Paul says this:

> Praise be to the God and Father of our LORD
> Jesus Christ, the Father of compassion and the
> God of all comfort, who comforts us in all our
> troubles, so that we can comfort those in any
> trouble with the comfort we ourselves have
> received from God.[1]

God comforted me in my pain by sparing my life, as I've
said! And He also comforted me by providing for me the
medication that enabled me to take back control of my
mind. Certainly I am alive; I was spared death, the one
final and everlasting good-bye perhaps to communicate
with you right now. You cannot fully know what God
is doing by allowing your suffering; He asks you just to
trust Him in it.

I must say here that I truly believe that, should you
decide to make a suicide attempt, you will experience
deep remorse and regret either this side of heaven if you
survive or on the other side, when God reveals the truth
of what He was trying to work in your precious character

through the suffering. Recall what Joni Eareckson Tada said, that your character is all you will take with you when you die. Should you die from the attempt, I believe that you will feel regret on the other side as well, when Jesus reveals to you what you would have experienced in later years had you persevered.

Who knows—in my case, perhaps the discovery of my delusions was just around the corner, as I've mentioned. Satan laid out before me an alternative to persevering that felt right at the time. So I took it and forfeited a future as an ambulatory person that I will now never know. Yes there is remorse and sadness, but as I trust God—that is all I can do—He continues in Romans 8:28 fashion to bring good out of what Satan meant for my ultimate and complete annihilation from the earth forever.

How Will You Spend Eternity?

At the time of the jump, I almost faced eternity. I'm very glad I didn't because I believe that a person who ends his or her life has to contend with some sort of diminished eternity as a result. I truly believe that there may be a direct correlation between how much you reached to the LORD while you were on the earth, and the quality of your eternity, including the depth and quantity of the "treasures in heaven" for which you will be rewarded.

It is said that there are levels in heaven relating to how you will spend your eternity, that how you relate in eternity is representative of how you related here on earth, and how you related to God in your suffering. Did you let Satan waste your suffering or did you surrender it to

God to be used for His glory? Did you complain and sit in self-pity or did you reach for, seek, ask, and knock on the door of God's heart in your suffering?

I said to a friend years ago, prior to my injury, that when we reach our own individual Judgment Day, we will have wished we had suffered more. It is through sur-rendering our suffering that we develop something that nothing else can accomplish—Christ-like character. I for one crave Christ-like character, since it's all I will take with me, and I believe that it will help me relate better to Jesus for all eternity when my time comes.

Chapter 23: The Vulnerable

Those who are particularly vulnerable in society come in many forms: the young, the old, those struggling with addictions, the disabled whether the disability be physical, psychiatric, or developmental in nature. I think we can find that these folk bring out in us our own painful vulnerability; they can get us in touch with our own deep pain.

We can seek to aid the vulnerable, to help them, but suddenly we can find that they are actually helping us. We approach them to be of service only to find that they are being Jesus to us in their brokenness. Recall Jesus' words, "I tell you the truth, whatever you did for one of the least of these brothers of mine, you did for me."[1]

I sense sometimes that seeing me in my weakened condition gets some in touch with their own vulnerability, which in turn can put them in a state of discomfort and can make them feel ill at ease. I remember Charles Stanley's words that life is not about ease, comfort, and pleasure, but about God growing you up into the likeness of His Son, as I have just spoken of in the previous section.

Recall that Jesus was broken and spilled out, that He

made himself so vulnerable for you that you may enjoy eternal communion not separation from the one who is love. He allowed Himself to be mocked, mutilated, and murdered just for you. Vulnerability at its essence has Jesus in it, for Jesus embodied vulnerability at its core, surrendering His body, His reputation, His very life so that the Father's Will could be fulfilled. Jesus willingly embraced weakness and made himself vulnerable for the Father's ultimate glory. Can we learn from and follow his example?

Just Like You

Do you have a particular weakness or vulnerability that causes you to feel like you are "different" in some ways, maybe in major ways? Perhaps you feel like you just don't fit in, that you're "special," that people in general don't hesitate to react to you that way. Let me assure you that I have felt these feelings. I felt unwelcome in my own family as a child. I even felt as though I had to somehow justify my very existence. Being now in a wheelchair aggravates these wounds.

Being physically disabled, certainly, there are so many wonderful people who help me readily when I ask. Sometimes, however, I feel that people coming up to me and asking me what they can do for me just accentuates and highlights my disability, my vulnerability. I can understand that seeing me, people may be naturally drawn toward wanting to help me. This is wonderful, I'm sure, as it shows compassion and a reaching out that is admirable. I wonder, however, if that person might also be feeling somewhat ill at ease with my disability and the way it makes him or her feel inside. Or perhaps he or she, feeling awkward, is just thinking that offering help is somehow the best thing to do. Don't get me wrong. I feel very grateful for people helping me. Where would I be without those folk who readily reach up on the high shelf in the grocery store to get for me some cappuccino yogurt, my favorite! I just appreciate it if they would wait until I ask them. I have heard this from other physically disabled people. Everyone needs to spend some time with a disabled person and learn to relax in his or her presence; perhaps then one can more readily come to grips with that little vulnerable part inside of him or her that's triggered at the sight of me in a wheelchair.

It may seem right to offer a token gesture to those who are different in some way, whether they be in wheelchairs or not. But, such folk as these really need your time and energy, your friendship. I find I am particularly connection-hungry being in a wheelchair. I value so much when a person engages with me, when he or she "enters in," as I've spoken of earlier, and asks me how I am and means it, is real with me, treats me like I'm like everyone else, does not immediately shy away because they feel, by looking at me, unbearably vulnerable (I refer you here to my poem, *Vulnerability*).

Granted, it may take some time to adjust to being around someone in a wheelchair; I understand this. Again, I encourage you to hang out with a disabled person and find that he or she, that people like me, are really like anyone else, like you, except that he or she may have, for example, nerve damage to the spinal cord.

If you are in a wheelchair or have other characteristics that seem outstanding, just remember that you are a unique individual like no one else. Your outstanding feature just makes you more outstanding, more unique, more special in a good way. If you experience rejection because of this feature, know that God loves and embraces you just as you are. We are all one-of-a-kind, but in the most important ways, we are so alike. We all have dreams and desires. We all need love; we all need the Creator to shower His love on us, His creation, in ways that fit our uniqueness. Won't you open up to Him and let Him do this?

The Family

Sometimes, however, it's difficult to find the love we need within our own family. The dysfunctional family is a smaller unit of a society of fallen people. Especially if that family is without Christ, how broken it can be. Yet with education and help, that family can pull together to help an ill member; that's what I've witnessed. As God has empowered me to just love the members of my family, not criticize, not reject, but accept and embrace them, God has done amazing works of healing.

As I show them love and appreciation through the Holy Spirit, they have grown to the point that we can come together and feel respect for and from each other. Through prayer and as I seek Him, God performs miracles in my heart that they see. He prunes and grows fruit of which all can partake.

I do thank God for my family. I am proud of how

far they have come with me and let them know it. I'm proud of the way they are steadfastly supporting me in the ways they can. I acknowledge that they tried to reach out to me in my psychosis. But like many of my friends at that time, they did not know just what to do. Forgiveness, which I've spoken of in the first chapter, is paramount as I process my disappointment and my pain to release them from blame.

Perhaps you come from a dysfunctional family where people are on polar opposites and cannot manage to see eye-to-eye. Embrace them as people made in the image of God. Love them unconditionally and watch as God works in their lives and in yours.

My mother certainly helped me fire the psychiatrist I had when I jumped, as I've said; with her help, I got a new, effective one. It was through her encouragement that I was able to take the stand that inevitably got me the proper treatment for my delusions. The new one, Dr. Edward Kingstone, not only diagnosed the condition but prescribed the appropriate medication for me finally after eleven months of psychosis. In addition, Dr. Kingstone came in the evenings to visit me in the rehab centre and remained, until his retirement, a steadfast support for me both in terms of counseling and the medication.

You may be a relative of one who is psychiatrically ill. As I've said in a previous section but reiterate because it bears repeating; you have a part to play to help protect and guard that ill one. Please take this role seriously. When that one is ill, making decisions and deciphering reality may be difficult for him or her. When one's mind is not in his or her control, the mentally ill can do some crazy things.

For instance, allow me to describe my state of mind at the time of the jump. When I became a Christian, I learned to rely on the Holy Spirit. This is how I came to make decisions. I did not grow up with someone with whom I could readily discuss decisions, so when I met Jesus and learned about testing the spirits, I felt I had come upon the answer to my confusion and loneliness. I would ask God for an answer to a question, then I would test the spirits, asking the answer if it proclaimed "Jesus as LORD" according to 1 John 4:1–3, as I've outlined earlier.

At the time of the delusions, my psychiatrist denied me counseling, so I was left with no one to talk to about the world I lived in. John Nash, in the movie *A Beautiful Mind*, developed, through a dialogue with his doctor, an understanding about his delusions.

On the day I jumped from the bridge, I heard a voice say that I had lost Rob, the man that I was dating, and the man I believed would be God's intended husband for me. I assumed this occurred because of my own foolish choices. I tested the spirits and felt assured that it was truly God's Spirit saying that. I also gathered that it was actually God telling me that I had lost His divine future for me where I would marry Rob, have two children with him, have a sailboat, horses, a farm, and be millionaires. It was this delusional belief that drove me to take my life.

All this to say that you cannot guess what is going on in the mind of one with a psychiatric illness. If you are the relative of one with mental illness, know that an advocate is necessary, so that in the case of acute illness, the ill one has a fighting chance to get the proper treatment. Do take that role seriously. As family, you have a responsibility; as I've said, you are your brother's keeper.[2]

Clearly the family plays a crucial role in the health of its members. Certainly as well as with psychiatric disorders, physical ailments can require advocates. I speak specifically of those with psychiatric illness not only because that's what I know but because he or she, especially in times of acute psychosis, is unable to advocate for himself or herself. Please understand the extreme vulnerability of the psychiatrically disabled, in particular. Remember that your loved one's very life may depend on your intervention.

Humility

Because of the difficulties I had had in my family and in my life, at one point prior to my injury I boasted, "I have a PhD in life." I thought I knew deep suffering. I had had the troubled childhood with the dysfunctional family. I had been through depression after depression to be raised up to study and produce at a graduate level. I had had a child in a bizarre set of circumstances. And I had read *Night* by Elie Wiesel, a firsthand account of someone who had been through the Holocaust. I felt I had educated myself about others who had undergone severe suffering and that I had, in fact, been through it all.

Jesus says, "For whoever exalts himself will be humbled and whoever humbles himself will be exalted."[3] Through my paralysis, I have had my eyes opened to suffering I had no idea existed. I reiterate that I experienced firsthand that which I believe breaks the heart of God: psychiatric patients in acute illness being turned away from their source of help, which they desperately need; the mistreatment of the physically disabled housed inappropriately in institutions; those with spinal cord injuries given merely three months to adjust to their disability and being expected to find housing for themselves when their very homes are inaccessible; marginalization, cultural rifts, and prejudices in the way the disabled are treated, as examples.

Have you been humbled by an experience that God has brought you to? Remember, if He brings you to it, He will bring you through it. I truly believe that once again He has proven to me that He is God, vast and immeasurable, and I am not. He begs me to let Him be God in my life. He asks me to stop second-guessing Him but just to trust Him. Can you let God be God? Can you just humbly trust?

Chapter 24: On Scripture

Getting to know Scripture is so important, especially for the time of acute illness of any sort. Grief blindsides a person, as well as those close to the sufferer. Sometimes, finding the right words to say to the sufferer or to his or her relatives and friends can be a real challenge. It is crucial to study, even memorize, Scripture, especially in the good times, so you can develop an arsenal to help you through the desperate days of a particularly heavy heart.

On the Love of Christ:

> And I pray that you, being rooted and established in love, may have power, together with all the saints, to grasp how wide and long and high and deep is the love of Christ, and to know this love that surpasses knowledge—that you may be filled to the measure of all the fullness of God.[1]

Certainly, we see evidence in the Scripture of Jesus expressing his love in many ways, as He performed miracles and showed compassion in his everyday living. He loved as an example, saying, "As I have loved you, so you must love one another."[2] Could He still be loving us in His divine way by allowing us to go through severe hardship and toil? Recall my favorite verse, "For my thoughts are not your thoughts, neither are your ways my ways," declares the LORD."[3]

I would suggest from this that Jesus experienced emotions, love, not only on a human level, but given his 100% divinity on an eternal level. Jesus' love, for example, is not only human but divine. Indeed the love that comes from God the Trinity is supernatural in nature. We cannot fathom the way God wants to love; that's where faith comes in. He asks us just to have faith, just to trust His incomprehensible brand of love.

I would go so far as to suggest that God not only has an eternal kind of love for us but also experiences eternal sadness. When we hurt ourselves, through a suicide attempt or even in small ways by belittling and demeaning ourselves, I suggest that He is sad in a way that is unique to Him, for He is eternal and we are His creation—finite.

We are His creation with whom we are in relationship. Just as a parent can be hurt by pain in the life of his or her child, God can experience hurt, I suggest, as well as love toward us, in a similar way. The added dimension with God is that He also experiences love and hurt in such a way that we cannot fully comprehend, given His eternal nature, and in light of Ephesians 3:18–19, quoted above. To sum up then, I believe that He loves us in an eternal kind of way that is somewhat foreign to us and conversely, hurts in an eternal way when we attempt suicide or even when we give fuel to the devil's lies that corrode self-esteem.

I reiterate that the second greatest commandment in Scripture is "Love your neighbor as yourself."[4] Learning to love oneself in a healthy way includes not only disregarding attacks on our self-esteem by the enemy but acknowledging that as a child of God, you are viewed by Jesus the Creator[5] so lovingly, with eyes that see beyond your flaws and weaknesses to your potential. He sees you in such a way as to model the way that we are to view ourselves. If we can but look to Him and embrace our identity in Christ and not look to others comparing ourselves, diverting our gaze from Him.

The Scripture[6] speaks about the depth of God's love for us, that nothing can separate us from it. His love in you is of such a supernatural and divine nature that going on one more day to experience this and to forge treasures in heaven[7], as I have mentioned, is an opportunity that should not be bypassed. Cling to Him who is love and to His amazing Word of love today and watch as He works.

On the Body:

I reiterate: "Do you not know that your body is the temple of the Holy Spirit, who is in you, whom you have received from God? You are not your own; you were bought at a price. Therefore honor God with your body."[8]

As a Christian, God lives in your body in the form of the Holy Spirit. If you are suicidal, know that you are not your own to take. You were purchased by Jesus. You were drawn to Him by the Holy Spirit. It was God who revealed the truth to you so you could step into relationship with Christ. Your body is the storehouse, the home of God in you. You need to worship with your body; destroying it is not honoring God.

I ask you: did you make your kidneys? Can you do what your liver does for you? Can you do without your intestines? Do you keep yourself breathing at night? God is at work in you in ways which you likely do not often think about and may even take for granted. I encourage you to study about the human body, to expose yourself to the workings of this wonderful creation of God, to develop a deep sense of awe and respect for the miracle that you call "you."

Scripture says, "For I am fearfully and wonderfully made."[9] That truth has never been more clear than when I lost the innervation to my legs, my bowel, and my bladder. My roommate at the institution said, "You don't miss the water 'til the well runs dry."

Recall other Scripture, including these words of Jesus: "The thief comes only to steal and kill and destroy; I have come that they may have life and have it to the full."[10] The evil one craves destruction whereas Jesus is the author, creator, and sustainer of life, on earth, and in the hereafter: "All things were created by Him and for Him. He is before all things, and in Him all things hold together."[11] It is clearly the devil's work to destroy; filling our minds and hearts with Scripture by reading and meditating on it, even memorizing it, as I've said before, can give us untold ammunition against the attacks of the enemy.

Other Prophets

Scripture speaks of others who fell into despair. Prophets such as Moses,[12] Jonah,[13] and Elijah[14] had been suicidal. In Elijah's case, God instructed him to eat and drink. Elijah needed food to revive himself; he also took some rest.[15]

Job cursed the day he was born rather extensively.[16] He spent many chapters expressing his feelings, getting his anguish out to try to make sense of what had happened. He did all this despite the inadequacies of his "comforters," for they tried to suggest that what happened to Job was a result of some kind of sin in his life.[17]

If you are low and finding that those around you are not understanding, if you feel bold enough to confront God, remember Job. The LORD's response to Job's query of Him was: "Brace yourself like a man; I will question you and you shall answer me."[18] Be prepared for a tough answer, if one comes at all.

In His response to Job, the LORD also expressed and elaborated on His greatness, on His bigness: "Where were you when I laid the earth's foundations? Tell me, if you understand. Who marked off its dimensions? Surely you know!"[19] We need to keep His majesty in mind when we are facing something that seems unbearable. Remember that God is eternal; our finite minds were not made to comprehend or grasp God fully. His ways are higher than ours. As well, He may choose to remain silent if and when you question Him about your suffering. Allow yourself to sit with the tension of God's ultimate mystery.

Recall that Job prayed for his friends, and "the LORD made him prosperous again and gave him twice as much as he had before."[20] Remember what God did after Job endured his trial: "The LORD blessed the latter part of Job's life more than the first."[21] Job gave God the chance to re-bless him. Won't you?

Try not to get stuck in the feelings of the moment. Certainly Moses, Jonah, and Elijah all got passed the feelings associated with suicidal ideation. Indeed they and Job were all mighty men of God, proving that no one, even those very close to and favored by God, are immune to deep despair.

Comforting Presence

Maybe you are or have been at the end of your rope as had happened to some of the other prophets in the Bible. As I've said, Job had his friends blaming him in the midst of his suffering. Perhaps you find those around you to be faithless, far from a comfort. When you suffer tremendously, remember that you are not alone. Let the presence of God be your comfort. He is there with you even when you don't feel His presence.

When suffering is relentless in nature, it is then especially that we must cling to the anchor, to the rock of our salvation, Jesus Christ. We must work through but not trust or lean on our feelings. This is not easy when "why" questions flood our minds, and we are tempted toward bitterness. But just know that He knows, He created you, and He allowed you to be tested in this way for a wonderful purpose, which He will, in His time, reveal to you. Perhaps that will not happen while you are on this earth, but He will use your suffering for His own glory if you surrender it all to Him, as I have said.

The rest of the human race has also had their share of trouble. You may feel alone; you are not. No one is immune; no one escapes suffering. Recall the words of our LORD, "In this world you will have trouble. But take heart! I have overcome the world."[22] I repeat this verse often because you really need to get into yourself that trouble is to be expected: "Dear friends, do not be surprised at the painful trial you are suffering, as though something strange were happening to you. But rejoice that you participate in the sufferings of Christ, so that you may be overjoyed when his glory is revealed."[23] Those, like me, who have been raised in a form of "isolation," emotionally and spiritually, or who are living disconnected from their loved ones can feel most alone and vulnerable in their troubles, like they are the only one going through such deep waters. When we are disconnected with others, we can, in fact, feel and stay entirely overwhelmed when trouble comes our way, concentrating on the unfairness of the situation. When a traumatic event happens to us, it's natural to feel overwhelmed, but we need to go to Jesus in order to move beyond these feelings and find healing and a restoration to wholeness. Seek Him who knows you, who indeed, knows all, and who yearns to be connected with you, who desires to be your friend. Rest assured that He can be trusted. He is, after all, one acquainted with great pain: "He was despised and rejected by men, a man of sorrows, and familiar with suffering."[24]

I too spent many days overwhelmed, crying out to God particularly in therapy. With the support of a godly therapist, I was able to visit, explore, and express deep pain in myself and invite Jesus to minister to me, to soothe my broken and shattered emotions back to a sense of wholeness and manageability. I learned to allow the dynamic relationship of give and take; I would give Jesus my wounds and would take from Him healing and comforting presence.

Chapter 25: A Dynamic Relationship

In a relationship, when one party hurts, the other party can be hurt for them by virtue of the very existence of the relationship. So it is in a relationship with Jesus. It can be dynamic, which is defined as energetic, active, and potent. (I refer you here to the poem, *Angry*.) I believe He hurts when we do, He rejoices when we do, He mourns when we do. And He weeps when we try to take our lives. Attempting suicide is referred to as hurting yourself. With God living inside us as Christians, we not only hurt ourselves but God who resides in us.

It strikes me that Jesus made us: "Through him all things were made; without him nothing was made that has been made."[1] He knows us better than we know ourselves; He knows our hurts, He knows our situations. He knows your situation.

The very best thing I can advise is to hand your pain over to Jesus, the creator and sustainer, the omniscient one. Let Him fight for you. (Recall *Footprints* referred to earlier.) For when we attempt suicide, when we don't give Christ the chance to work in our lives, we are attempting to destroy God's creation,[2] which He said was "very good,"[3] which is God's possession[4].

Allowing God to come into your damaged emotions with hope and healing is so important. In fact, it has been revolutionary in my life. After I was injured, I ran to Him in repentance, and slowly He took me and made it cope-able. It was about 4½ years post-injury that I was able to embrace real peace about my injury, as I was clearly seeing God work in my relationships with my family and friends, even with strangers that I would meet and influence because of Him. Attempting suicide can be you expressing, "He can't!" and "I won't let Him!" Oh, how we need to go to Him, lay ourselves bare before Him, asking Him to heal and comfort us as only He can! Oh, how He longs for us to do this! In fact, He may have put you in your current circumstances just for that purpose, in order that you would run into His arms!

When I tried to take my life, I gave no thought to how Jesus would react to my doing so. I thought I knew best. In the story of the Prodigal Son,[5] I wonder what the father felt when the Prodigal Son went from him with his inheritance and squandered it. It doesn't say in the Scripture, but I can speculate that it was profound dis-appointment, betrayal, sadness, even rage. He felt some-thing, after all, he was in relationship with his son.

As I've said earlier, I imagine that the father must have worked through his difficult feelings to be able to welcome his son back when he returned home in such a celebratory way. Not all of us have people directly in our lives with whom to work through our feelings; this was the case for me, at least when I was a child. To help resolve difficult feelings, I sought a therapeutic relationship in terms of a godly counselor where I learned to invite Jesus into my pain, thus deepening my relationship with Him.

Now I take time to recall just two of the Father's rich promises: "'For I know the plans I have for you,' declares the LORD, 'plans to prosper you and not to harm you, plans to give you hope and a future;'"[6] and "being confident of this, that he who began a good work in you will carry it on to completion unto the day of Christ Jesus."[7] When I attempted suicide, I thought nothing of these.

In fact, I took my inheritance of salvation and presumed upon it, squandered it you could say, like the Prodigal Son did of his monetary inheritance. God did not receive me into heaven, but instead, disciplined me for His glory. He taught me what a suicide attempt can do, how suicide is so, so serious. As I've said, I ran back to Him after I was injured and gave him my pain. I decided I was going to let Him work in my life as He saw fit, not demanding my own way. He, in turn, welcomed me back as I got up and got back on my horse.

Life with Jesus can indeed be a dynamic relationship. I pray that you may be given the strength to cling to him in the very midst of your storm and that you can hear the words, "Quiet! Be still!" just like He said to the storm when the disciples were afraid for their lives.[8]

I see suicide now as a turning away, a lack of trust, a closing the door in life's face, indeed, in Christ's face, since "all things were created by him and for him."[9] If He created you and knows all about you, if He wanted you in heaven right now, He could arrange that. But He has called you to this suffering for a profound and eternally deep reason that only He knows fully.

Attempting suicide is saying that Jesus doesn't know what He is doing in our suffering. I encourage you not to give up. I urge you to press on into life, incomprehensible though it may be, with Jesus. Don't turn away from allowing His mighty hand to work in your life and circumstances. Remember, keep your eyes on Him, not on your circumstances.

You Can Never Take it Back

Circumstances can grow and grow when we focus on them; this can cause us to be more at risk to act on suicidal ideation. Remember, you cannot ever take it back. A serious suicide attempt cannot be undone. If it is successful and you do not know Jesus as your Savior, you will suffer eternally, indescribably more than you are suffering now. If you survive, regardless of whether it maims or not, the suicide attempt takes a deep toll on our confidence in ourselves and in God, as well as on those around us. You can be inundated with shame. You can wonder whether you have it in you to go on after an attempt, particularly if you gaze at your circumstances in the natural or look to yourself instead of to Jesus to resolve the situation. Those around you can be so disheartened. It can, as well, encourage another weak brother or sister to further contemplate or attempt suicide.

It can weaken your faith and the faith of those around you. Friends and loved ones may seriously question your ability to handle life and may seek to overprotect and coddle. Following an attempt, it can be so difficult for the sufferer as well as for his or her friends and loved ones to go on. Yet, moving forward in your present situation may not seem so impossible if you think about what it takes to fall and get back in the race.

I do not say that there isn't mystery involved in what God allows. Recall my favorite verse, "'For my thoughts are not your thoughts, neither are your ways my ways,' declares the LORD."[10] Certainly it talks in the Bible of God making a ruin,[11] as I've said, and that Christ's Second Coming will usher in destruction,[12] for example. The Bible, in addition, speaks of the sinner's destiny. The LORD will punish with "everlasting destruction."[13] The word destruction in Hebrew means something similar to complete ruin.

My point is that God sometimes even allows destruction in lives, that He is not afraid to discipline and discipline harshly. Recall, "The LORD disciplines those he loves."[14] Though I was not in control of my mind at the time of the jump, I believe that God did discipline me, especially with this last suicide attempt. He took me and let me see suffering that I never dreamed existed, both personally and socially, in terms of the mistreatment of the mentally ill and the physically disabled, for example. I say again that He also opened me up to the seriousness, the ramifications of trying to take one's life.

Certainly He has taught me more about Himself. Yet this seems a very harsh way to teach me these things. Could there not have been a softer, kinder way to teach me, I wonder? Could not my delusional state have been diagnosed and treated without this devastation in my life? With God, there is mystery, as we cannot see the eternal perspective. Perhaps He has put me in this position precisely so that I can relate to you. Are you in a position where you feel disciplined by God? I say again, "The LORD disciplines those he loves." Like a loving father toward his disobedient child, discipline can be done because of love, not in spite of it.

We need to come to a point where we just rest in faith, resting in Him knowing that one day we will be shown the full picture. We may even receive glimpses of His mind, His reasoning, while we are here on earth, but patience is required because we will know completely only on our day of Judgment.

As I lead someone in the Sinner's Prayer or speak to an audience about my struggles and my faith in Jesus, I get a glimpse of His reasoning. Yet there are days when I think about the complications of the paralysis, the difficulty with travel, for instance, and I can be thrust back to a time when I am wondering why once again. This doesn't happen as often as it did when I was newly injured, but still, the questions come some days. I can't take the suicide attempt back; I have to be satisfied with these glimpses of His mind. Are you feeling regret for a decision you made that cannot be undone? I understand.

Yet trust Him to solve and redeem your pain in ways that are higher and greater than you with your finite mind can conceive: "Now to him who is able to do immeasurably more than all we ask or imagine, according to his power that is at work within us, to him be glory in the church and in Christ Jesus through all generations, for ever and ever!"[15] He is able! Trust that!

Chapter 26: On Free Will

Certainly there is the issue of free will that He allows suicide, because He has given us free will. Free will, however, assumes a certain degree of mental health and the ability to make decisions. When you are not in control of your very mind, as can be the case where mental illness is concerned, a person is in a very dangerous position indeed. Help is required at that point, help from an outside source, help in the form of a compassionate and skilled doctor, other health professional, or advocate.

Are you facing a situation where you need outside help? Are you seeking it but not getting it? Are you exercising your free will as much as you can to try to access the help you need, all to no avail? It can be very challenging indeed to be in need of medical care of any type in this day and age.

I see the psychiatrically ill not given the treatment they need, having to stay in medical wards because beds in the psychiatric ward are not available. I see people in grave and obvious need having to endure lengthy waits in the emergency department, sometimes resulting in death. Again in my case, my inability to access proper health care significantly contributed to my near-death experience.

Nonetheless, the consequences of the suicide attempt are as real to me now as for someone who endures paralysis for another reason. To this very day, I carry the paralysis as a reminder to myself and to others of the seriousness of making an attempt to end your life. To be honest, I have to give thanks for the paralysis as, it was actually through the disability that I was able to get the proper treatment for my mental illness, when, as I've said, a more experienced psychiatrist, Dr. Kingstone, diagnosed the psychosis that other professionals had missed for so many months.

Jesus is a gentleman; He will not force himself on anyone. (I refer you here to my poem, *A Gentleman.*) Perhaps I wanted someone to literally step in and save me. Maybe you are feeling this way. Jesus sends someone or does the healing Himself on some occasions, not all. Remember that Jesus healed many, not all. Because He may not have healed us does not mean He is not active or sovereign in our lives. I reiterate that His ways are not our ways.[1]

He allows us to turn away and can bring ultimate good out of suicide because that's just how awesome He is, in true Romans 8:28 fashion. A little over six years after the injury as I've said, about forty people began a personal relationship with the LORD because I am in this wheelchair—my bus drivers, friends, acquaintances I only just met. I had, at that point, been able to tell my story on radio, on TV, and in speaking to the public educating them about my experience with depression. Now I am using my will that is truly free, as my mind is now healed from illness, to dig into God and let Him use me and my suffering as He chooses, as I follow Him in prayer, in faithfully reading the Bible, and in memorizing the Word.

His whole book, the Bible is, in fact, one big exhortation based on the fact that He has given us free will, assuming one can absorb it and glean truth from it, something I found very difficult indeed while psychotic. Once again, in the case of psychosis, an advocate is needed to bring the ill one's mind back to sanity so rational decisions can be made. The entire Bible was produced to help us make right decisions, to guide, strengthen, and comfort us in our times of struggle and pain. We are not just pawns in a game of good versus evil; we have a part to play. Certainly, even the psychotic person, if suicidal, has a part to play. He or she needs to be able to articulate that he or she is in crisis and reach out for help.

Recall Paul's words:

> "For our struggle is not against flesh and blood, but against the rulers, against the authorities, against the powers of this dark world and against the spiritual forces of evil in the heavenly realms. Therefore put on the full armor of God, so that when the day of evil comes, you may be able to stand your ground, after you have done everything, to stand. Stand firm, then.[2]

Clearly these are instructions to us with free will: we have a part to play.

Though he railed against the very day of his birth[3] and wished he had died at birth,[4] Job did not speak of ending his own life; he did not have the belief, it seems, that that was an option open to him. He had a will that was free to the extent that he could choose how he handled what God allowed; he was able to vent his pain, to share his pain, even though his comforters did not seem to understand. This is so important, to be able to verbalize and express our feelings in the suffering.

Perhaps there are support groups and counselors waiting to listen to you, you with your heavy heart. Perhaps the story of Job tells us that it is not so much the reactions of the comforters that matter as much but that they were willing to listen and absorb and allow Job to have his say. I offer you this once again: if Job had committed suicide, we wouldn't have the book that has helped so many through the centuries, and he wouldn't have had the chance to receive the blessings God poured out on him near the end of the book.[5] Certainly, as I've mentioned, Job received not only spiritual blessings from enduring his suffering but added material ones as well. God may not bless you with things, but I know that He is at work in incredible ways spiritually in and through your suffering as you choose to let Him have His way in and through it—in ways that only the suffering can produce. A prayer of Moses in Psalm 90:12 is one that I have put to memory and has been such a comfort to me especially in times of trouble: "Teach us to number our days aright, that we may gain a heart of wisdom." I pray this for you as well.

God allowed Satan to tempt Job, so God does allow temptation, but I believe that that allowing and our free will are inexplicably bound together. We are being tested; our faith is being tried by fire, the "refiner's fire."[6] Perhaps God is searching you to see how you will respond to His trial in your life. Certainly God knew that I would be driven in my mental illness so far as to want to kill myself, but maybe He allowed that too for His reasons, glimpses of which I think I have seen, as I have said. Certainly the paralysis has afforded me the ability to relate to others in agony where, prior to the injury, I would not have had the words.

Suicide, I felt, was an acceptable way of coping when one had reached one's limit, when one could bear no more, when he or she could not go on for one more day. Or could he or she? One needs to break time down when one is suffering greatly. Travel on your journey inch by inch, hour by hour, minute by minute if necessary. Life is created by God and is of infinite preciousness, as I've said. You are of infinite preciousness. You are unique in all of creation. No one has the same fingerprint or heart-beat as you from now and for all eternity. You were "fear-fully and wonderfully made,"[7] crafted by God Himself, an original.

Just think of how far both God and you, with your free will, have to come to get to where you are now. You had to travel over many peaks and valleys to get to the point where you are reading this. Just think of how you have struggled. Again and again, you may have chosen the path of life in the past. Don't sell yourself short. Remember your and God's faithfulness, how He has seen you through already so much.

A friend said, "Yesterday is dead and buried, and tomorrow is too far away." Gazing too far ahead or too far behind can be a real danger. To look into the past in order to find resolution for hurt feelings is one thing, to stare and be fixated on it is another. Paul says, "Forgetting what is behind and straining toward what is ahead, I press on toward the goal to win the prize for which God has called me heavenward in Christ Jesus."[8]

Choose to live in the present, pressing on to the future: Chuck Swindoll, in his book *Laugh Again*, said that God is not in yesterday, then He would be, "I was." God is not in tomorrow, then He would be "I will be." But God is in the now because His name is "I am." Let God comfort you where you are today. Use your free will to soak in the Word, to commune with Jesus in prayer, and to talk with Him, listening for that still, small voice, strengthening the relationship between you and He. He's waiting with open arms to receive you in *this* way.

Chapter 27: Physical Comfort and Happiness

Given our free will, we can choose our direction. When physical comfort and happiness are the goals in life, we find it more difficult to embrace suffering when it comes. Life to me at the core is not about comfort and happiness. Certainly, as I've said, Charles Stanley says that life is not about ease, comfort, and pleasure. It's about growing into Christ's likeness. Happiness is a byproduct of serving the LORD. It need not be a goal.

Service

Originally I thought it would have served me better in the temporal, which is all I can see, being able-bodied. I could get around with greater ease, and be spared all the relational difficulties that go along with being in a wheelchair. But recall Paul's words,

> But whatever was to my profit I now consider loss for the sake of Christ. What is more, I

> consider everything a loss compared to the surpassing greatness of knowing Christ Jesus my LORD, for whose sake I have lost all things.[1]

Being disabled now, I can share in the sufferings of Christ, thus communing with and relating that much more with Him. Do you think that your sufferings can get you even better acquainted with and more understanding of our dear Savior?

Life is not about me, as Rick Warren says. It's about God, by whom and for whom I was made. If I were still able-bodied, I truly believe I would be more self-serving. I would seek more to meet my needs rather than be aware of Jesus and the needs in others. It is through my paralysis that my faith has grown, and my ability to see Jesus everywhere, as I've mentioned, has developed.

Now I see Jesus all around me. I see His suffering in ways that I would have previously missed, purely because my faith has grown. Faith, as I've said, is the bridge between the temporal and the eternal; it is the muscle that lies between these two joints. And it is this widened faith that spurs me on to good deeds and service to the "Jesuses" I see around me. Can you give your suffering to Him and let Him develop this muscle called faith inside you, faith that leads to fruitful service? Another good verse to put to memory is James 2:26: "As the body without the spirit is dead, so faith without deeds is dead."

Assuming

Especially one contemplating suicide needs to have a

good sense of where they will go after they leave this earth. Assuming on God has sealed an eternal destiny of doom for many, I'm sure. Assuming that God will honor them as "good people" who lived "good lives" and therefore should go to heaven has likely prevented many from accepting Jesus and asking for forgiveness.

Satan is called "the prince of this world."[2] He offers the pleasures of this world, luxury, comfort, and ease. I notice that those who have been left alone by him and have the goodies of this world lavished on them may be in a very perilous situation spiritually. There were psalmists who wondered why the wicked prosper and the righteous suffer. I believe that success in the world may be offered to those who have this world and worldly success in mind—expensive cars, lavish homes, big bank account. Charles Stanley says that in the end, this amounts to ashes. What is built for the kingdom is what truly lasts. Certainly Rick Warren says that life is but a preparation for the next. How many have been satisfied with earthly pleasures, unaware that storing up treasures in heaven[3] is really what's needed?

The devil also suggests that your good works will outweigh your bad ones, that this will get you to heaven when you die. He promises a works-oriented salvation, as religion offers, where being a good person and doing good deeds will gain you entrance into heaven. How many who have committed suicide have assumed that only to face the ultimate destruction when it comes to his or her Judgment Day?

Jesus clearly states in his word, "I am the way and the truth and the life. No one comes to the Father except through me."[4] Charles Stanley asks if Jesus is a liar.

Christ also says, "I tell you the truth, no one can see the kingdom of God unless he is born again."[5] Either He was lying or the inerrant Word of God is wrong. Truth can be difficult. Certainly life is difficult. Face life in all it's difficulty and complexity. Embrace the truth of Jesus Christ. If you are a person without faith, don't assume that because you've lead a good life that that alone will be rewarded with entrance into heaven. I sincerely hope that you don't find out the truth when it's too late. I encourage you to make a decision to follow Jesus and receive the forgiveness that He paid such an incredible price to deliver to you.

Chapter 28: There Can Come a Point

Suicide is also a decision. And it's a decision, which, as I've said, you cannot take back. I do believe there can come a point at which we decide to carry out our plan, where we're through with talking, where a decision has been made.

I suggest to you that such a decision is made on inadequate and inaccurate information. In my case, it was made when I did not have an adequate grasp of my reality. I found myself at a point where I had no more energy to reach out, where it seemed like the only option for me to take my life based on the delusional beliefs that I had lost God's fantastic future for me and that I was a failure to God. Neither one of those things were true, but I could not see truth at that time. Just to say that there may be another perspective other than the one you have about your suffering.

You may be at a point where you are still listening, still seeking input, are still in the process of making your decision. Please mark this: if only you could see yourself and your situation through God's eyes, if only you could see His purposes and reasons for allowing what you are going through, if only you could feel His compassion, His tender love for you at this time in and through your pain, you might find some peace and contentment, rather than the tossing and turmoil you may find yourself in, teetering on a decision. I pray that the gentle love of Jesus could reach you before you come to a point when you're through listening.

I would add that because the Father decided that His one and only Son would die the most painful and agonizing death so as to redeem all of humanity, surely God knew what He was doing when He decided to allow your suffering. Remember my favorite verse that states that His ways are not our ways.[1] Allow the God of mystery to still reign in your heart. Choose life, choose Jesus, every small step of the way.

Collaborative Effort—Definition of "Self"

When one ponders suicide, he or she may think that it is himself or herself who is the only one involved in the decision to end his or her life. By the word "self", one might think of a single entity perhaps in three parts: a body, mind, and soul. But I contend that self is made up of a collaborative effort of all the people who have helped us, not to mention our Creator. "For you created my inmost being; you knit me together in my mother's womb. I praise you because I am fearfully and wonderfully made."[2] God is ultimately in charge of all that we are physically. He can allow anything to go wrong at any time; there is Someone bigger in control. Won't you acknowledge that?

You are also a compilation of the love and attention your parents and siblings and friends gave you—your teachers and influential secondary folk as well. Sometimes we can have a meeting that changes our lives, something someone says sticks in our minds, or a loving gesture or thoughtful act touches our hearts.

Perhaps there were those who supported you in prayer, if not in other ways. We are not an island; we are interconnected, all of us. We are in a web that involves others. We are who we are because of a collaborative effort. People are waiting and watching; take your role in the web seriously. We need each other's strength and courage interdependently. I need your courage; to see it inspires me as it does others.

Self, then, is made up of not just one person, I contend. It is a blend of all the influences in our lives. Certainly we carry with us part of the hearts of each person who cares about us, and certainly those people's hearts will not ever be the same if self chooses premature death.

Relentless

When those close to us have mistreated us, years of ill treatment reinforce a pattern that becomes automatic in the mind of the victim. It can cause a person to be seriously critical of himself or herself as the person unconsciously recreates either in reality or in his or her mind the abusive environment that he or she calls home. The enemy can create a cycle of inner abuse that is so relentless in nature that there is no rest; he kicks a person when he or she is down. A victim of abuse can be so relentlessly hard on himself or herself, giving fuel to the "tapes" that condemn, that he or she will stop at nothing to denigrate him or herself.

Internal abuse can be relentless in nature, so we who are prone to this must be relentless in our pursuit of Christ. We must find Him by seeking and asking and knocking and keeping this up until the Spirit breaks through with light and love, enough to help us not only to forgive ourselves and our perpetrators, but to find His hope for our future. In the spiritual war we are all in, we must be as relentless as the enemy can be, looking to the Savior and His example to find victory: "May the LORD direct (our) ... hearts into God's love and Christ's perseverance."[3]

A Blessing Not a Burden

We need to be relentless, not only within ourselves, but also interpersonally, being mindful and diligent in conveying loving messages to others, particularly to the vulnerable who are especially prone to negativity.

I said to a friend that I did not want to be a burden to him as I was going through deep, dark waters. He responded, "You're not a burden. You're a blessing!" That was the first time I had heard that. Sometimes as a child, I felt like a burden to my parents who were harassed by life's trials. Certainly, now in the wheelchair, I can still sometimes feel like a burden in social situations. Did you ever, do you ever feel that way?

Often we can feel that way unconsciously with God.

We tend not to pray to Him because, for instance, we were received by our earthly parents with impatience and frustration. We are already at a disadvantage before we come to Him. Deep down, we can fear God will react the same way, not have the time or energy to give to us. Are you hesitant to approach God? Is praying, communing with Him a real chore? Prayer is work. Nonetheless, God can replace our heavy hearts with His "easy yoke" and "light burden"[4] when we come to Him finally.

What about that vulnerable one in your life? What message are you sending to him or her? Are you revealing to him or her through your words and your actions that he or she is a blessing or a burden? All particularly vulnerable people, such folk as the elderly, the young, the disabled, and the weak need to feel that they are a blessing. What are you doing to help those people around you like the ones I've listed here to feel like they are a blessing? What are you feeling if you fall into one of these categories?

Know that regardless of how you feel because of the actions or words of others, you are a blessing to God. You are His creation that He called "very good:" "God saw all that he had made, and it was very good."[5] Don't allow the enemy to lie to you that you are not infinitely precious and a blessing in His sight. And you, strong one, share the wealth. Give from your heart and the spiritual riches that come from Christ to help those lesser ones around you feel special and blessed. As you give your heart to others, God can give you spiritual riches.

Chapter 29: More On Job

I say again that Job cursed the day he was born and wished for death, saying: "May the day of my birth perish[1] ... Why did I not perish at birth and die as I came from the womb?[2] ... Or why was I not hidden in the ground like a stillborn child, like an infant who never saw the light of day?"[3] Despite these very heavy feelings, he persevered.

Job spoke at length, he tried to verbalize what he was feeling and going through, despite the fact that his "comforters" blamed him and were not very comforting. This is a lesson to all of us that it's not as much even the reaction of those near us that matters, as the fact that they listen and absorb, that we get the chance to verbalize our feelings.

Even when Job spoke to God near the end of the book, God's response was to speak at length about his creation and His power; Job responded that he was "unworthy,"[4] finally saying,

> I know you can do all things; no plan of yours can be thwarted. You asked, 'who is this that obscures my counsel without knowledge?' Surely I spoke of things I did not understand, things

too wonderful for me to know.... My ears had
heard of you but now my eyes have seen you.
Therefore I despise myself and repent in dust
and ashes.[5]

Job was humbled and awed in his conversation with God.
He then expressed regret and turned from his ways. Then,
as I've previously highlighted, "the LORD made him
prosperous again and gave him twice as much as he had
before."[6] Job's perseverance resulted in change, a change
that worked out for the better. Remember, the only constant in life is change. Though he could not go back and
reclaim his original status before the calamity, he grew
from it and was blessed more so than before. Unlike Job,
we may not experience material blessings, but we will be
richer spiritually through endurance as we surrender our
trials to Jesus, as I've said. Our faith will deepen, and we
will enjoy deeper fellowship with Christ here on earth
and when we see Him in eternity.

God allowed Satan to torment Job; God may be allowing you to suffer to test you. Understand that it is an act
of one's will, an act of passion to step out and actually try
to kill oneself. If we can but diffuse the passion a bit by
talking and expressing that which lies buried as Job did,
we too can find God's deliverance and freedom from the
feelings that drive us to suicide.

On Lies

It is true that suicide is an act of one's will. It is a facing of
death. Though suicide takes courage, it reveals a dedica-

tion to a series of lies that say things cannot improve, that you are not going to feel differently about your suffering in time, that suffering does not serve an eternal purpose. Christ-like character is hard to come by; it is through suffering that He wishes us to reach to Him in humility and repentance. However, one can suffer innumerable trials and remain bitter and hard-hearted, closed off to help, including that of a divine nature. It was through Jesus' suffering that redemption was bought; suffering has a redemptive quality to it. If we go the distance, God is faithful to bring us through. We need but to endure by clinging to Truth and to the promises of God. Endurance itself has a way of bringing new insight, new perspective. It begs us to dig, to do emotional and spiritual work to try to understand. It calls us to look up; it can cause us to contemplate what death will hold. We can try to grasp eternal things. Suffering is the spur God uses to cause me to gallop to seek answers in Him, to gallop towards Him. Don't listen to and act on the lies of the enemy, but look up to one who knows all. Christ will give you the strength to face the truth: recall that Paul said from a jail, "I have learned the secret of being content in any and every situation. (So it *is* possible) ... I can do everything through him who gives me strength"[7] (amplification mine). Truth is things will change, as I've said in the section above, as you continue to seek Him with all your heart.

Love Endures

As you choose to go on and endure, you can sow love.

Love is patient, love is kind. It does not envy, it does not boast, it is not proud. It is not rude, it is not self-seeking, it is not easily angered. It keeps no record of wrongs. Love does not delight in evil but rejoices with the truth. It always protects, always trusts, always hopes, always perseveres. Love never fails.[8]

Love endures. Loving acts endure and will come back to you for all eternity.

As you choose to carry on, you will have more opportunities to do loving acts and therefore, you will forge a deeper and richer eternity for yourself. Suicide by its very nature is an act of impatience that demands, "Make it better now or else." It can be an act of defiance against the fact that "life is difficult;" it is not an act of embracing this as fact. It certainly is not an act of love. Go on to sow love, it endures.

Idealization—Black and White Thinking

Extremes in thinking can make sowing love a real challenge. I realize that I have, in my life, idealized people to be much better than they actually were or I idealized in reverse, fantasizing them as being terrible ogres. I believe this came from my lack of connection as a child. I lacked the intimacy of another human being in order to develop a more healthy, more balanced view of others.

Perhaps you have been living with extremes in thinking. This can be very painful, as it creates isolation or the opposite, dependency, as it did for me. Reach to Him who yearns for an honest relationship with you. Share your heart with Him and listen as He speaks to you. Prayer can be a dialogue of a deeply intimate and healing nature. As you reach to Him, you can learn to rest in His presence. It can lead to reaching out to others. It can lead to a sharing with others, building trust, and learning to articulate feelings. A therapeutic relationship was so helpful for me at this point, as my black and white thinking made it difficult for me to make and sustain friendships; I found I would develop extreme views of people I had only just met.

A healthy therapeutic environment helped me foster intimacy in safety without the fear of rejection as with a normal friendship. This I found particularly necessary since emotional safety was absent in my early years. I reached out and made a deep connection with another human being in a healthy therapeutic environment; this provided healing slowly for the extremes of black and white thinking as I was able to make room for gray areas.

Chapter 30: Trying Too Hard

As well as having extremes in thinking, not seeing other human beings realistically, I can have a tendency to try too hard. What I mean by that is this: the little girl inside of me who lacked consistent healthy connection and consequently never matured properly is still in her immature way trying to work herself toward acceptance by others. Because my heart could not rest in a pool of acceptance and gratitude for being loved, the little girl strives, motivated by fear of rejection. She doubly fears rejection because, as she did not feel accepted early on, it only takes a hint of rejection from another to trigger this core reservoir of hurt. She holds so much stock in what others feel about her, again since she lacked a foundation of acceptance.

Sometimes she almost expects and often unconsciously seeks rejection because it is what is familiar and known. She craves acceptance but really feels at home with rejection; it's what she deserves, she feels, because that's what she felt, at times, from her primary caregivers. They, after all, must be right. She hangs on to those feelings, which hamper her growth. She believes she is not worthy of true love, so when it comes, she does not know how to receive it. It feels so foreign to her, like a pauper wearing silk. Her efforts to relate have to transcend this core of hurt, so she ends up trying what others see as too hard. It's a vicious circle because it is this trying too hard, trying to make up for inadequacies and earlier rejections, that tends to put people off and can actually lead to rejection itself.

If you are realizing that you are a person who tries too hard, rest assured that Jesus accepts and embraces you fully. He knows all about you, all your weaknesses and disabilities, and loves you just as you are. I have found great healing in receiving Jesus' loving embrace for me. I have in my bedroom a picture of Jesus cradling a wounded lamb. He is holding that lamb so closely to His breast. When I look at it, I think of how He embraces me every minute. Indeed, I am never alone and never unloved, though I may not always feel it. As I rest in faith, in His open, welcoming arms, I can experience the love and acceptance I crave; He truly satisfies my soul. He makes me feel whole. He causes the little girl inside to rest, to cease striving; He lifts her heaviness. He can do it for you too. Bring the pain of that little one inside of you to Jesus and watch as He takes you up in His arms and comforts you with His love.

Keep Your Eternity in Mind

Even in and through our suffering, Jesus can satisfy our souls, as I've said, which are not temporal but eternal. I repeat: our souls are eternal. In light of this, I encourage you to keep your eternity in mind. Remember Jesus enduring his suffering gave us the Savior of all mankind. He won a spiritual battle. Suffering has a spiritual, eternal quality to it. Eternity is an unfathomable thing. So it is that we are sometimes called to unfathomable suffering—suffering beyond our scope to understand. In order to forge an eternity, Jesus acts or allows something that we might feel is unreasonable, for He is, by His nature unreasonable (by finite, human standards) and incomprehensible. Recall that He is, at His core, mystery.

It strikes me that God had to make eternal restitution. He had to make eternal compensation for Adam and Eve's decision. He had to annihilate sin on an eternal level—that's why so much suffering. Not only did God the Father have to compensate for Christ's humanity but he had to make restitution for the divine eternal side of Christ. We cannot comprehend the eternal so we will never fully comprehend God's plan. That's where faith comes in. We can rest in faith, knowing and believing that God has it all in His control. God had a plan not only for Christ but for our lives—a plan that has an eternal component to it that we will never fully grasp with our finite minds.

God knows and sees your eternity; He has a perspective that you and I will never see in this life, as I've said. Believe that God will use suffering in your life or even suffering in another's life to try to bring you closer to Him and to forge for you a deeper eternity. He knows it sometimes takes drastic steps to bring you to Him, and He will stop at nothing to do just that. He knows that there is nothing better than for you to commune with

Him; He knows that you would want that too, if you truly understood.

Jesus entrusts certain suffering to you because he hopes you can use it as a catalyst to promote growth in your faith and in your intimacy with Him, which you will enjoy for all eternity. As I've said, I do believe that there is a direct correlation between the time we spend with Him here on earth and the quality of our eternity. Seek Him now; you will thank Him later, perhaps even for the great sorrow that you bear that has dragged you to your knees.

He cares for you so much that He's willing to go to extreme measures to get your attention, to cause you to sit up and take notice of His infinite and sovereign power in your life. He knows His character in you will last forever, that is the only thing that will. Remember: He cares for you in an eternal way that is unique. Sometimes we feel exactly the opposite and ask: how could God allow this or that to happen if He loved me? Recall that His love, His ways, His thoughts are all incomprehensible to our finite minds;[1] His brand of love we will not fully understand this side of heaven. God knows all; He ultimately is more concerned for your eternity than for your comfort. Try to keep that in mind.

Chapter 31: Intrusiveness

Jesus is a gentleman. His love is non-intrusive. He does not force us to speak or do anything; He merely waits until we are ready to come to Him. Waiting is what He is, since He is love and "love is patient"[1] first of all. We can learn from His depth of patience.

The dynamics between my parents when they were newly separated was understandably very tense. Witnessing my father's disdain for my mother from age four, I withdrew from my mother, for fear of "betraying" Daddy. My Mom, on the other hand, frustrated at this, would tend to insist that I tell her, for instance, what was bothering me. I, in turn, learned to be intrusive. I couldn't see the boundaries of others. I would tend to think that what I thought was showing caring was actually intrusiveness.

Again, I don't mean to harp on this, but I cannot stress enough the enormous help good counseling has been for me, both personally and professionally; it was in a therapeutic relationship that I learned healthier boundaries. I came to recognize my need, for instance, which was previously unconscious, to try to encourage in a prodding kind of way, self-disclosure from friends, as well as professionally, from clients. Friends would be turned off because I would not allow for a gradual build-up of trust and a slow unfolding of issues and self-disclosure. As a result, I had many "friendships" with people who felt more sorry for me than were able to truly love me as a person. With clients, it was me taking the lead instead of keeping a cardinal rule of counseling, in letting the client lead.

I believe I was intrusive, I tried to "force" trust in a way, because I was starving for connection, and was desperate to help partly because of my parentification. I was intrusive also because of a lack of understanding that issues naturally unfold as trust is built in time.

I realized finally that trust, something so very fragile and precious, must be married with patience, a quality that God is abounding in. It was through counseling that I realized that trust blossoms, in any relationship, including a therapeutic one, as I take the "gentlemanly" stance of our Saviour to watch and wait for someone to come to me emotionally and spiritually. (I refer you again to the poem, *A Gentleman*.) In relationships, whether they be personal or professional, I can offer encouragement to share when he/she is ready; however, I need to follow Jesus' example and behave respectfully with regard to the boundaries of others. If you can relate to this section, be gentle with yourself. Learning appropriate boundaries can sometimes take a lifetime; sometimes it takes good help too. I still can fall into the pitfall of intrusiveness, but I am less prone to doing this simply by virtue of my awareness of this tendency within me.

Uncomfortable Truth

My boundaries with Jesus involve a tension with God, tension because I seek to understand Him and am sometimes frustrated because His eternal nature eludes me. I want to know all the answers right now. Can you relate? I seek to understand Him, especially with my therapist in the institution, Paul. I find I get angry at the way Jesus reveals the truth and at the truth itself that I am confronted with especially in therapy. I know I've had a good session when I become angry and reticent at Paul for leading me to an uncomfortable truth.

Perhaps you feel this way at God or at a truth-telling friend, loved one, or therapist in your life. Perhaps you have someone in your life who tells you not what you want to hear but the Truth that is sometimes so tough to bear. Truth is, "Life is difficult." Jesus, grant us strength to receive Your Truth for us and to embrace it eventually, as You say that it is the very thing that "will set ... (us) free."[2]

Leisure/Workaholism/Intimacy

The truth is that my mother was concerned with the cultural development of her children. I saw my first Shakespearean play at age nine. We would go to ballets and other cultural events. I was encouraged to take piano lessons, swimming lessons, and ballet. As well, I went to camp a number of times as a child and in my youth. All of this helped me to develop culturally and socially, and for which I am very grateful. However, we did not have regular down times with the family just for fun or for the bonding of it. We did not go on holidays or have outings for dinner, at least partly though, because the money was tight. In addition, the scapegoating I experienced actually drove me away from my family.

It was when I was in my teens that I was embraced by a group of young people who accepted me as I was. It was with them that I grew in my ability to be more social with people; they helped me come out of my shell and my withdrawal to some degree. Yet deep intimacy eluded me. For many years I felt that marriage was out of the question for me, especially since I had only known my parents, my primary model of an intimate relationship, as expressing deep disdain for one another.

I learned to bury myself in work. I tended to disregard leisure, some of which is so important if we are to achieve a healthy balance of work and play in our lives. My father had a strong work ethic, so I embraced and found solace, actually learned to hide from intimacy with others in my work, leaning towards workaholism. Later on, when I became a Christian, intimacy with God, for instance, was difficult as I would avoid specific and concerted times of prayer.

Perhaps you have not been exposed to a lot of bonding times within your family. This can add to a feeling of heaviness when we become adults. As a result, we may not have been able to learn to be socially intimate, to *feel* intimate, to feel free-flowing love and respect for one another, which can be such a strengthening, relaxing, and renewing experience.

Running from social intimacy, I was driven. I even felt guilty when I was not producing. Taking time out left me with discomfort and made me feel ill at ease. Maybe you too have escaped into work or soothed your discomfort at intimacy with productivity. As I've said, this can contribute to if not produce a feeling of heaviness.

Developing intimacy with Jesus is so important in the healing of a heavy heart. Listen to His very words:

> Come to me, all you who are weary and burdened, and I will give you rest. Take my yoke upon you and learn from me, for I am gentle and humble in heart, and you will find rest for your souls. For my yoke is easy and my burden is light.[3]

Learning to lean on and be spiritually intimate with Jesus, the vertical, in prayer can help us so much. He can teach us to reach then, to the horizontal as well, to other Christians in fellowship, for our need as humans is for both the horizontal and the vertical. Practice intimacy with our LORD by disciplining yourself to do concerted prayer times, scriptural meditations, and regular Bible reading. Reach out to fellow Christians and don't run out right after church but join in on fellowship times and in small group meetings. I say especially to those of us for whom deep intimacy was not fostered in our childhoods, we need to practice reaching out to embrace newness and the rewarding experiences involved in deep relationships with God and with others. Take heart and gather your courage to forage into perhaps unknown territory. Developing spiritual intimacy with God and interdependence with others is essential in the healing of a heavy heart.

Chapter 32: On Prayer

Someone said that it is not when things are going well that we search for someone to thank, by looking to the vertical, for instance. It is through trial and despair that we can find ourselves reaching up. God is calling us to deep fervent prayer. Suicidal despair is a gift that speaks to the urgency of seeking God. It also calls us to community, for it is when we are in despair that we desperately need the prayers of others. Job himself said, "A despairing man should have the devotion of his friends, even though he forsakes the fear of the Almighty."1 Prayer, in fact, can be so difficult when we are in despair that we can turn from God; it is in these times that we especially need a praying community.

I remind you here of Paul's writing to the Corinthian church, when he and Timothy had "despaired even of life."2 At this time, Paul said, "On him (Christ) we have set our hope that he will continue to deliver us, as you help us by your prayers."3 He openly entreated the Corinthians to pray for him and for Timothy. The prayers of others can be such a vital support as we go through the process of our suffering. As I've said, this is especially helpful when we find it difficult to pray. If you are feeling this way, you can ask God to give you the strength to reach out to Him and to His people.

In my own personal prayer time, I find the more I pray, the more God brings to mind things to pray about. And God is not like our earthly parents, who were limited in patience and time. Unlike them, God is available "24–7–365," as Danny Brooks sings. There isn't a human on the planet that can keep that type of schedule. Sometimes, as I've said, when approaching God we can hesitate, thinking He might not take the time or have the energy to commune with us, especially if we were given those messages as youngsters. Sometimes it is so hard to pray because our unconscious transfers these early interactions with our earthly parents of not being received with patience and acceptance onto God. Believe me, God is just waiting with open arms to commune with you in prayer. It is the gateway to true intimacy with God.

Go to him, just as you are or as the song says, "Just as I am." That's how he accepts you, warts and all. Don't feel embarrassed or that you've got to jump through hoops to please Him even before you approach Him. His love is higher, deeper, richer than the love we have received here on earth from others. Go to Him, just as you are. He'll embrace you and love you whole as you share with Him your pain.

Many times it's just sheer perseverance alone that gets us through, a sheer determination to hang in there. When our situation surrounds us, Satan can tempt us with such thoughts as, "what's it all for," and "how could you allow that, God, and say you love me," the "what if's," the "if only's," and the tormenting "why's." This is why, by an act of the will, we need to set our hearts and our minds on things above.[4] It is also an act of our will to seek out God in things that can encourage: books, videos, music, exercise, others who uplift and do not drag down. Certainly we need to seek God's wisdom in regards to how and with whom we spend our precious God-given time. A song on the "*O Brother, Where Art Thou?*" soundtrack says, "There's a dark and a troubled side of life; there's a bright and a sunny side too. Keep on the sunny side." Negatives can spiral us downward. By not dwelling in them, but letting them come and go, we can stay spiritually afloat. Let Christ and His divine optimism buoy you up. Remember and memorize Romans 8:28: "And we know that in all things God works for the good of those who love him, who have been called according to his purpose."

By an act of will, we also need to turn to that which is in our control: prayer. When we feel powerless in situations beyond our control, we can take the power back by entreating the one who has the control: Jesus. Prayer can be therapy with the Great I Am. It involves a spilling out, a sitting back and a listening.

Jesus can speak to you countless times throughout a day. Learn to be sensitive to hear that still, small voice; as well, bring your burdens to him. Prayer is the key to life: it brings joy and releases feelings of helplessness and hopelessness, as I've said. It is something we can do when all else is beyond us.

Being suicidal represents a desperate need to pray and to be prayed for. Often, however, it can take a great deal for a suicidal person to pray, to reach out in any form amidst the onslaught of what feels like a driving need to die, as I've said. Ultimately, we need to acquiesce to the fact that His ways are eternal[5] and out of our grasp to fully comprehend. We need then to rest in faith, that at Judgment Day, we will know all and until that time, we need to trust that God is in control, persevering until we see Him. Truly, to be able to pray is to be free.

Responsibilities

Prayer is so important, because as long as we are on this earth, we will have responsibilities, sometimes very heavy ones. We will always have the responsibility for caring for ourselves as adults; if you are a parent, you have that added, tremendous responsibility of caring for another human being. As we surrender our responsibilities to Jesus in prayer, He can offer His direction and strength. Even children have responsibilities, perhaps with pets, to do their chores and to help out around the house.

Sometimes keeping up with responsibilities can be daunting and difficult indeed. Perhaps financially you have debts and you find it difficult to keep up with all the expenses. Perhaps you have been left alone to go on without your partner, or perhaps you have struggled with what feels like an overwhelming load of care for as long as you can remember, even from your youth. Perhaps you, as a child, were asked to support your stressed-out parent(s) or be forced into a role of peacemaker when the family was in turmoil with fighting. Or perhaps you are a caregiver to a relative with serious health problems. Maybe it's *your* nagging health problem that hinders you from full enjoyment of your day. It can be these relentless responsibilities that can contribute to, if not create, a heavy heart.

Children who are burdened with care can recreate that type of emotional environment for themselves as adults. If parentification, for example, was an issue in childhood, the adult may unconsciously involve himself or herself with people who want to be taken care of. That hurt, that reservoir of pain, if unexpressed, remaining repressed, can end up running the life of the wounded one.

You cannot control what happens to you, but you would be surprised as to how much control you can take over the way you handle your spirit and your emotions, which comprise the seat of your soul. It is your responsibility to learn how to communicate your feelings without being merely reactive or accusatory. Practice saying things like, "When you do or say _____, I feel _____," rather than "You make me feel _____."

Learn to own, to take responsibility for your feelings. For me, being raised in quite a dysfunctional family, I seek the safety and additional guidance of a counselor in order to learn to appropriately express myself. I do have other excellent relationships but it is in therapy that I can practice and learn more social skills. This professional needs to be a person who creates an accepting environment in which I can "swim", whatever my feelings or attitudes. I needed to shop for a good therapist, one with whom I clicked. It took time and effort but it was worth it; a good therapist to me is worth his or her weight in gold. As I've said, I choose a godly, praying therapist who brings the Holy Spirit in as the third Person in the counseling session.

Journaling feelings can be helpful; I can even use journal entries as fuel for a counseling session. Learning to articulate my feelings took practice; I tried it with trusted friends as well as with my therapist. Where possible, using humor and levity lightened the way and rejuvenated. Talking to God about feelings, I have found, can provide deep release as well. Remember no one knows you and understands you quite like God does. And as I've said, God is always available. In those times that I have felt that I have needed someone to talk to but no one is there, I have indeed proven that God's grace is truly sufficient.[6]

We may, however, feel we need someone with flesh on them to cling to. Another person is good for feedback, for others can see things in us that we do not see and can help us gain insight. However, to cling to another is co-dependency and idolatry, which is contrary to the first commandment: "You shall have no other gods before me."[7] The only one God wants us to be dependent on is Him. I may need others more now that I'm disabled, but that just translates into a greater dependency on Him.

Remember, your feelings, your hurts are ultimately your responsibility. You can allow them to stay repressed and live in denial, or you can face them bravely in prayer, perhaps in counseling or with trusted loved ones and friends. You can surrender them to God and watch as He heals and performs miracles in your heart as only He can do.

Direction

Truly, as He performs miracles in our hearts, we can get a glimpse of His eternal purposes for our suffering. And even if we don't get this glimpse while we are on this earth, surely, one day, we will know all:

I was on the WheelTrans bus, and I thought he said he'd take the highway, so I was looking forward to a speedy ride. He didn't take the highway but a slower road. I was frustrated and asked him why he had changed his mind. He said he didn't change his mind that we had to detour for another pickup. So I let go of the highway. I was frustrated not to be going fast in wide, open spaces, but now I understood. It was easier when I understood.

We went into Queen's Quay and picked up. Then he drove along that street instead of the Lakeshore, a more used roadway. I was frustrated and I wondered why. I was about to ask him, but instead, I choose to just let that go too, as I could see we were getting to our destination. It was better when the destination was in view.

We finally got there in good time. In hindsight, I could see why he took the roads he did. All became clear; I no longer questioned him or felt angry at the seemingly quick and odd turns. It all made sense and I breathed a sigh of relief.

Chapter 33: Every Little Bit Counts

Originally I didn't want to do physiotherapy. To do fifteen minutes of pedaling on an arm bicycle hardly compared to the many lengths I used to swim and the long walks I would go on. I would compare what I did then as an able-bodied person with what I can do now, being disabled. I felt forlorn. But slowly, as I came to physio more and more, I would feel a lightness in my spirit. This, for me, is exercise.

With this new insight, I then sought to do as much physio as I could. I would make regular use of the Motomed (the motorized leg bike), arm bike, and pulleys, for that is my exercise and every little bit counts. I believe God will honor that.

Now, being out of the institution, I travel over an hour one way to go to a fitness centre for people of all abilities. I do this twice a week, using a Motomed, arm bike, weight and leg machines adapted for people in wheelchairs, and I wheel around the track for forty minutes. Exercise is one of the best ways that I can get a lift.

In the spring, summer, and fall, on the days I don't go

to the fitness centre, I wheel up the street for about forty minutes. In addition when I go to the mall once a week, I take time to do a forty-minute wheel. In winter, I use a theraband, a piece of stretchy elastic that I can pull with resistance on the four other days when I cannot wheel.

Exercise is so important, especially for those with heavy hearts. It has a way of generating energy and dispelling depression. With feelings of despair and suicidal ideation, go little by little, hour-by-hour, minute-by-minute if necessary, because, as I've said, every little bit counts. As you put a trickle of energy into your well-being, God can take it and flood you with His strength and His blessings. He is right there with you with every effort you make.

The Way We Die

Sometimes when we feel deep despair, as I've said, we need to inch forward minute by minute. I reiterate: no matter how it happens, with suicide, there is a shroud of shame and dishonor associated with it, not only for the person himself or herself but for the family of that person. Everyone questions why the person couldn't have been helped to go on one day at a time. Emotions in those around the person who attempts suicide, like guilt, rage, and grief are exceedingly difficult, and it is easy to lay blame. The way we die is important.

If we die with victory and honor, there is a legacy of pride and relief for those left behind. As well, others develop an admiration for the person who stuck it out to the very end. We admire a person who endured suffering until God chose to call him or her home; there is a sense of closure that comes more quickly, a resting, a peace for others with someone who has endured to the end.

Though we may not fully understand the reason for our suffering, we need to come to a victorious death by resting in faith, by reminding ourselves that Jesus has everything in His sovereign control, that He knows what He is doing both for our good and for the good of those around us.

As I've said, by an act of will, we need to train ourselves to think of good things.[1] We need to take steps to help ourselves out of the despair that can engulf. I say again: God asks us to do a great deal. He asks us to work hard for stability. As I've said, plow a field and leave it that way and weeds grow. Buff silver and leave it, tarnish grows. Leave fruit long enough and mold and bugs come. A rolling stone gathers no moss, they say. Even the seemingly smallest of efforts can in time be translated into overflowing energy and strength in the hands of a loving God.

We are asked to work diligently in the midst of our despair, to seek Jesus and His will. Though it may seem monumental, take that first step with God to reach out beyond your despair. Remember, it is up to us ultimately to seek the care we need. Seeking to stay in Jesus' will, we can never go wrong. It's important—the way we die. Make the choice to reach out if and when you find yourself in despair. Don't allow the feelings to engulf you to the point of taking your own life. Choose to let God decide when and how your life will end. After all, your very creation was in His sovereign hands, let your death be as well.

Count Your Blessings

I've said this before, but it's worth repeating; an attitude of gratitude can make a huge difference in providing strength to choose to go on. "Giv(ing) thanks in all circumstances"[2] requires that we count our blessings. Believe me, there are more than you can name. I would encourage anyone to befriend a disabled person. This can in turn help you be thankful for what you have. To witness the tenacious spirit of a disadvantaged one in action can help you carry your own cross.

Perhaps God is calling you to volunteer in your local nursing home, hospital or long-term care facility. Take seriously the call to be with the "least of these." Recall Jesus' words, "I tell you the truth, whatever you did for the one of the least of these brothers of mine, you did for me."[3]

As you reach to the "less fortunate," God can bless you in ways that would surprise you. You may even find that the one to whom you go to minister ends up ministering to you. Reaching out in this way can fill you with joy and cause you to see more and more blessings in your life, blessings that were previously hidden or that you took for granted.

Psalm 77

One way to lighten your load is to minister to "the least of these." Another way is to work through your grief.

Psalm 77 is a real "working-through." The psalmist here takes great pains to identify and articulate his distress: "My soul refused to be comforted,"[4] and "I was too troubled to speak."[5] He feels "reject(ed)"[6] by God, that God's love has "vanished,"[7], that His promises fail.[8] The psalmist even asked God where His mercy and compassion were.[9] But then the psalm takes a turn. (I wonder if it takes a turn purely because of the work the author has done to articulate and express his deep pain.) The psalmist finds strength to engage faith and let it make a decision to "remember the deeds of the LORD ... your miracles of long ago."[10]

He works through his disillusionment and his rage and gets to the point where he makes an active decision to dwell on good things that the LORD has done. The parting of the Red Sea is mentioned; the psalmist also writes of the power of God displayed in a simple thunderstorm or an earthquake. Certainly we are all helpless before and at the mercy of God, as I've previously mentioned.

Can you identify and articulate with a trusted friend or counselor the feelings that threaten to engulf you? Can you find expression for these deep and troubling feelings? Can you then reflect on the good things God has already accomplished in your heart and life? Can you see His hand at work to bring you thus far? So far He has brought you, hasn't He? Remember this promise of God to you: "(B)eing confident of this, that he who began a good work in you will carry it on to completion until the day of Christ Jesus."[11] Can you believe it?

You need to do the work of allowing your feelings to come up to be expressed and allow faith to decide where you will go and what you will do in your despair, as seen here with the psalmist. Faith and trust in God cannot steer you wrong. You make poor decisions when

262 HOPE FOR THE HEAVY HEART

you turn from God. Charles Stanley says we need to take our eyes off our circumstances and stay fixed on God, for our circumstances only grow larger the more we dwell on them.

Life, Jesus says, is not easy. You will have trouble, and sometimes we can contribute to it directly ourselves. How often do we rush to do things without thinking and have an accident of some sort? Or we've failed to get enough rest or eat properly, and added weight causes health problems? Or we make ourselves too busy to fit exercise into our days and arteriosclerosis develops? Especially when we are in despair, our motivation for taking care of ourselves can dwindle, and therefore our physical health is more at risk. As I've said, I felt great regret and remorse for having indirectly caused my own spinal cord injury. If you've made a poor choice that has caused much pain, know that you are not alone.

We must work hard at seeking hope; we have choices over how we respond. Let Psalm 77 be a model for us in our pain. Express yourself thoroughly in a safe environment. Let faith win. We can stare downward or we can reach in and up. We can lose heart or "take heart" as Jesus said, when we are confronted with troubles. Which will you choose?

After SARS Confinement

My faith was strengthened through confinement, if you can believe that!

I was confined to the institution for four weeks during the SARS outbreak in March, 2003. And what an incredible sense of freedom I experienced when it was over! I thought then, "What tremendous freedom I will have when I get my new body in heaven![12]" I will have known what it is to be confined. I will have known "imprisonment", so I will know freedom that much more. (I refer to you here to my poem, *Freedom*, which I wrote just when the confinement ended.)

Chapter 34: Saying No

God gave me lessons today in saying no. No to the woman who curses and screams, no to the roommate who expects me to be always there for her, no to the woman who feeds me lies, no to the man who wants to complain to me about his woes and not work things through. "No. I cannot." It's hard to say it. It takes practice because I feel fear and guilt when I say it—fear of an angry response that may lead to withdrawal of love, and guilt from an expectation of being an endless source of giving, an expectation that is exaggerated by my having been scapegoat of the family and by my having been parentified.

The guilt is false, for God knows I'm not an endless supply of energy and compassion. God knows the fragility of my humanness. God knows I need to take as well as give. With a blurring of the boundaries within the members of the family as a result of enmeshment and with the feeling that I could not please my caregivers, I learned to give over and beyond what was healthy for me. My mother and father could hardly be expected to teach healthy boundaries since they did not possess them themselves.

Learning to say no is a real challenge for me. I would

allow myself to be used as a doormat for others. I lacked the ability to be assertive and therefore was abused. I lost my virginity to a date rape because I was easily manipulated into letting a stranger into my home. Learning to say no, though, is oh so necessary, if I'm going to practice healthy boundaries, since unhealthy ones can contribute, if not lead to a heavy heart. Learning to say no is necessary as well, to be able to let God help me protect and love myself, as I am commanded to do so many times in Scripture (recall Jesus' words: "Love your neighbor as yourself"[1]).

I am not Savior. He is. I am human, made of flesh and bones, breakable and penetrable, fragile and frail. It is He, as Savior and Creator, who teaches me that. It is He who also teaches me how to care for myself, giving me the permission and the strength to say no. Are you having trouble saying no? Seek Him and He will do for you what He has done for me.

Displaced from Home

Many of us, despite our frailty, take the reality of having a home for granted, yet when I was displaced from my place of residence, I found these words of Jesus especially comforting: "Foxes have holes and birds of the air have nests but the Son of God has no place to lay his head."[2] To know that Jesus was born in a stable, poor and "unwanted," that He died the same way, to know that the majority of his life he spent roaming from place to place without a "home" base comforted me as I faced the letting go of the beloved place I called home. If you have been displaced, remember that Jesus knows what you feel; consider Him your solace as you are forced to call a difficult place home.

Rick Warren, in his book *The Purpose Driven Life*, has said that in order to keep us from becoming too attached to earth, God allows us to feel a significant amount of discontent and dissatisfaction in life—longings that will never be fulfilled on this side of eternity. He goes on to say that we're not completely happy here because we're not supposed to be, that earth is not our final home. We were created for something much better.

Hang on if you have been forced out of your beloved refuge.

> Do not let your hearts be troubled. Trust in God; trust also in me. In my Father's house are many rooms; if it were not so, I would have told you. I am going there to prepare a place for you. And if I go and prepare a place for you, I will come back and take you to be with me that you also may be where I am.[3]

Rest assured that God is preparing a place for you in the very home for which your soul was and always has been intended. Hang on to that hope as you wait in patient expectation of the coming glory in His time.

This Life A Preparation

We may endure displacement from our homes; this and other suffering has caused me further to believe that, as Rick Warren says, that this life is merely a preparation for the next. Bad things happen to good people because it is these trials that God uses to mold something beautiful, to mold spiritual riches. This life is transient. As a song by Casting Crowns says, we are "a wave tossed in the ocean, a vapor in the wind." What would you rather have: loads of pleasure and comfort here or spiritual riches there? I see so many trade one for the other. After all, we are going to be spending a lot more time in eternity after we die. Do the seventy or eighty years we may live here on earth compare with eternity? God knows it doesn't. How could He be a loving God to indulge you in this life and not consider the other?

This world is said to be Satan's. As I've said, he is referred to as "the prince of this world."[4] The world is his realm; he promotes overindulgence, obesity of body, mind, and spirit, lavishing with comfort and pleasure. That is his domain. God has a higher purpose; God is concerned with your character—I reiterate that this is the only thing you will take with you when you die, as Joni Eareckson Tada says. Satan is concerned with the here-and-now. God is concerned with the sweet by-and-by. Thank God that we have a God who cares for us in an eternal way, though it is a way that we will never comprehend here on earth.

Satan argues that a God who cares is one who spares us from troubles. God knows we need them as coal needs pressure for it to turn into a diamond. He is preparing for us diamond characters to enjoy for all eternity. So hang in there! He has a purpose. We're not home yet. As I've said in the previous section, we are being prepared to go to the place for which we were created. Let Him prepare you in the way He chooses. Let Him decide when you will go home. He created you; let Him be Creator and Sustainer of your very life.

Interconnected

As Jesus prepares us for eternity, we can realize with greater clarity that we are all interconnected. Knowing of your triumphs encourages me as much as seeing your sorrow saddens me. Indeed, we are admonished to "(r)ejoice with those who rejoice; mourn with those who mourn."[5] Our hearts leap with those who achieve and sink with those who plummet.

I don't know of one person who does not feel sick when hearing about someone committing suicide, and if a person does not feel sick at this, I contend that that person himself or herself is disturbed in some profound way. Suicide leaves a hole in the interwoven tapestry of life—an irredeemable, unpatchable hole. Indeed, we are all interconnected. We need each other interdependently. Please don't go.

Have Patience

Have patience, please. God is doing something rich, something deeper than we can know in our suffering. I truly believe this. If we can but trust Him in it, and hang on, we will see that come our Judgment Day[6] it will all be worth it. We will be glad that we persevered when God reveals His reasons, His eternal perspective to us.

As I began the prose section of this book, patience

is what is required as we await Judgment Day when all will be made clear, when there will be "no more death or mourning or crying or pain."[7] Recall that "the first and greatest commandment"[8] is to "Love the LORD your God with all your heart and with all your soul and with all your mind."[9] And the second greatest commandment, "Love your neighbor as yourself."[10] Can we love Him, love our neighbor, and love ourselves with our patience? Please do. And I will too.

Poetry

Part 1: On Emotions

The Pull of Home

Happy or sad
Good or bad
There is a pull of home for true

Homelife beckons
And it reckons
To be recreated by you

If turmoil you did have
Then unconsciously for real
You may go around
Reliving the same deal

For it's very hard to know
To gain insight, to grow
Not to let the unconscious rule
You need to go to relationship school

For me, it was counseling
That helped me understand
How, for instance, I saw
My father in every single man

I find since turmoil was the norm
That I am at home in a storm
I did cling
To those that sting
As unhealthy relationships I did form

For home has a pull
That's deeper than deep
It'll run your life
It'll play for keeps

So Lord help me
To step out and be
Brave to take the steps
As beyond home I need to get.

Eternal Love

"God is love,"* pure love
But of an eternal kind
Not love quite as we know it
But unique, you will find

For sometimes what He allows
And what He does
Causes great pain
Doesn't look anything like love

He uses it to mold you
To draw you to Him
He bids you surrender
And let Him deeply in

He doesn't stop calling
'Til your life is through
He weighs all you are
And all that you do**

For He wants you to know
Him more deeply, Him more
So you can relate to Him better
When you get to that Heavenly Shore.

*1 John 4:16: "God is love."
** Matthew 16:27b: "(H)e (Jesus) will reward each
person according to what he has done;" Ephesians 6:8:
"(T)he Lord will reward everyone for whatever good he

has done;" Hebrews 9:27: "(M)an is destined to die once, and after that to face judgment."

A Plea in the Grief

So much to let go of
So much is lost
I've regained my mind
But oh, at what a cost

I feel a deep sorrow
A deep eternal sadness
Wonder if I will again
Live in God's joy* and gladness

Please God help me find
A life worth the living
Help me strike a balance
Between getting and giving

Help me find a place
Where the toil is worth the strain
Help me Lord, get up in the morning
Again and again and again

And say it's okay
Honestly
To find, to hold
Life's key

The key to life, Jesus
He makes it hopeful
Lord, make it
Realistically "copeful"

Please allow me to
Let You find a way
To find meaning and life
In living paralyzed day after day after day.

*Recall that about 2 ½ years post-injury, a friend referred to me as "Ellen of Joy."

Angry

In relationship I am
With the Great I Am
Make me frustrated You do
They call it angry too

For you show me things
I just don't get it
They're unfathomable, eternal
Sometimes I want to quit

It's a dynamic relationship
A moving towards and a moving away
And this back and forth
Can change from day to day

Sometimes I'm
Inexplicably in love
Praising You, my Saviour
Gratefully gazing above

Sometimes I'm angry,
Even hateful and have disdain
Because you show me things
That cause me great pain

But in the end
You have my freedom in mind
Your suffering is for my benefit*
Benefit of an eternal kind.

*Just as Jesus' suffering was for my benefit, and bought me eternal salvation, the suffering He allows in my heart is also for my benefit, making me a deeper, richer person and preparing me for the life in the hereafter.

Come Out and Be Strong

Living on the edge
The edge of despair
Climb out of the hole
Only to fall back there

I gain some ground
Then something happens

To plunge me back down deep

To where I struggle
To where I hide
Myself, my dreams out of reach

Where I go to hide
From the dust and the din
Can't feel Him near
Won't let Him in

This is familiar
I know this place
This was my home
Spent years in this space

But do I, do you, when you
Spend extended time here
Stamp on His grace
Instead of drawing near?

We all have bad days
He knows and understands
But try to remember what it's doing
To Him and all of your fans

Discourage them you do
When you choose to live in a shoe
Come out and be strong
You know, it hasn't all gone wrong.

Bitterness

It threatens to take you
It threatens to make you
Unforgiving, unyielding, hating, biting

It keeps you from you
It keeps you from me too
It keeps you from wrongs righting

Hate, hate
It cries
Destroy
Despise

It threatens to take your soul
It will swallow you whole
It is the worst enemy
From it, God, set us all free

It is the greatest foe
For it wants your soul to sell
Not the body but the soul
Into a living hell

Where it blocks out
That which is good
For it goes on a mission
Destroy and destroy it could

Destroy relationships
Friends, relatives, loved ones
Get out the knives,
The bullets and the guns

Destroy even yourself
It won't stop at anything
It'll make you its slave
It'll take your wedding ring

It eats away at all that's dear
It'll spread far those that are near
Beware I say beware
To dance extended with it,* don't dare

I think it's part of deep grieving** though
So if you feel it, let it come
But know, it must pass
To its grasp, you dare not succumb

Let this be a warning then
To you and all you hold dear
Don't hold on to bitterness***
But to God draw very near.

*Hebrews 12:15: "See to it that no one misses the grace of God and that no bitter root grows up to cause trouble and defile many."
**Proverbs 14:10: "Each heart knows its own bitterness, and no one else can share its joy."
***Ephesians 4:30-32:

"And do not grieve the Holy Spirit of God, with whom you were sealed for the day of redemption. Get rid of all bitterness, rage and anger, brawling and slander, along with every form of malice. Be kind and compassionate to one another, forgiving each other, just as in Christ God forgave you."

Drunk with Grief

I am drunk with grief
Drunk with despair
Social mores
I don't even care

I sing loudly and long
In the open sanctuary
When no one is there

I say to the crucifix
On the wall, "F--- you"
In full humanity, I do even dare

For I'm angry and bitter*
Bitter as can be
My blood boils over
It rages inside of me

I tried to find Home

My eternal one and true
Because my earthly one
Just wouldn't do

I hope there will come a time
When I'll be able to say
I've learned a lot, it makes some sense**
And live for Judgment Day

When all will be made clear
Was it my fault or theirs?
And once again I'll walk
Finally free of my paraplegic cares.

*I got over my rage and bitterness with counseling.
**Six years post-injury, I have helped over forty people come to faith in Jesus.

O Selfish God?

What a God
But a selfish one
Would take most of my life
Then ask me to go on?

He didn't save me, it seems
Or provide a way out
When all that was within me
Was bitter rage and doubt

The bitter rage persisted
Was as strong as it could be
Anger so vile
Deep inside of me

Anger for them
And for myself too
I hardly escaped
My inner wrath for true

For I killed myself
Or at least did try
A strong Christian too
Some say, "My, my, my."

Satan gets us down
And wants us to stay
In despair so long

He plants in our hearts
Seeds of destruction
That feel so strong

With mental illness
Recurring and relentless
To these feelings
We can feel defenseless

But just know that
Satan is a defeated foe
God can forge
Out of deep despair hope

For a human spirit
Is resilient for true
God is really there
For me and for you

To take all that's precious
And ask me to go on
Seems to me selfish though
Or could I be wrong?

What kind of love
Is that which requires
A stripping of all
That one hopes or desires?

A revamping of life
A restructuring too
Hopes and dreams revisited
He makes everything new*

Can I possibly say
That He knows what He's doing
Can I really just trust?

One sweet day
He'll make all things clear
Cling to the hope of that Day** I must.

*Revelation 21:5: "He who was seated on the throne said, 'I am making everything new!'"
**Referring to Judgment Day in Hebrews 9:27: "(M)an is destined to die once, and after that to face judgment."

Vulnerability

No one should be paralyzed
With this world being as it is
Fraught with anguish and pain

They say, "Life is difficult"
Even without the paralysis
Now it's doubly so and again

"Life is complicated"
"Life is unfair"
Now I have to live it
From this chair

Can't get around
Like I used to do
Can't relate so easily
From me to you

A social barrier
I find this wheelchair to be
Do you cringe deep inside
When you see me?

Do I remind you
Of your brokenness inside?
You know, the part of you
You always try to hide

No one should be paralyzed

But could it possibly be
That I am like this so you can see
Your own deep and fragile vulnerability?

A Heart Full of Love

Open your heart up to His
And you will find there
A heart full of love
To hold your every care

Open your heart
And you will see
That He'll give love
Oh so tenderly

He is the Master
At kindness, at love
Nothing can replace
What comes from above

For He will bestow
On any and everyone
Love true and pure
He asks you just to come

He takes you then
And breaks you down
He crumbles the heart of stone*

He replaces it
With a heart overflowing
With a soft one all His own

A fleshy heart
He will give
He will teach you
To really live

And love in ways divine
Please mold me and take me
Make me wholly thine.

*Ezekiel 11:19-20: "I will give them an undivided heart and put a new spirit in them; I will remove from them their heart of stone and give them a heart of flesh. Then they will follow my decrees and be careful to keep my laws. They will be my people, and I will be their God."

Part 2: On Relating to Others

Paralysis of the Will

I have a friend
Who's stuck in a rut
Deeply burrowed down

He can't find his way
He's wrapped in chains
Feels trapped within a frown

For he carries with him
Bag upon bag of care
In his unconscious
It's deeply hidden there

Just out of reach
Just out of view
God take him
On a way that's new

'Cause the weight of that baggage
It paralyzes his will
We try to help
But he persists still

In carrying his luggage

Not unloading and unpacking it
He's working so hard
He just won't quit

So help him surrender
It all, Lord, to You
So You can shoulder
And carry it too

For he's too strong to be weak
Oh help him to see
That You and I he needs
To live interdependently.

Ode to Pete

Burdened with a family
That don't know how to care
About the things that move Pete's heart
They really don't dare...

...dare to enter in
They stay on the sidelines
He's a psych. patient
That is his crime

They live in caves hiding
Live in busyness striving
Not offering a hand to hold

Inside they are distant, cold

For he is a mental patient
To them and always will be
Debilitated, struck down
Vulnerable and weak

Look down on him they do
As an equal he's not seen
In a psych. ward and a mental hospital
That's where he's been

So he's judged
For this illness of his
Not of his own making
But of God's, it is

Yet on solid ground
Pete stands on the Rock*
He seeks help from His Creator
And from his trusted doc

He works things through
When he gets tired or overwhelmed
He knows where to go
For help in the psychiatric realm

He's braver than he knows
He takes his illness and grows
He talks about his feelings too
All the right things he does do

Pete may be your neighbor
He's not so far from you
So look upon this man named Pete
You might just learn a thing or two

Think twice when you
Cross him on the street
He is truly amongst the most
Honorable men you could meet.

*See Isaiah 26:4: "Trust in the Lord forever, for the Lord, the Lord, is the Rock eternal."

Ode to Friends

I am disabled
Or paralyzed too
Take a moment, do an inventory
Look deep within you

For I may not feel
The ground beneath my feet
You know I cannot even stand

But with the friends God has given
I find I can fly as they
Reach out and lend a hand

With help, I can soar

Feeling interdependence
Is really such a feat

Where my strengths
And those of friends
Intermingle and meet

For I have friends
That empower they do
They give courage
En-courage me too

Thank God for those that care
Thank God for those that dare
To help me to flourish and grow
As beyond the surface they willingly go.

A Connection

They work in the institution
And everyday they find
Overwhelming needs

Each day they come
Many can do little more
Than the basic physical deeds

Many come in and out
Just doing the physical task

They cannot engage with me
I have to wear a mask

A mask that says I'm okay
They don't talk with me today
Their minds are so full
Of their own aches and pains

Because the needs in this place
Are so overwhelmingly huge
Some find it hard to smile
And face the day as new

For I am the needy
Am I spurned too?
Spurned for my vulnerability
I touch a part in them I do

That part in them
That makes them feel small
That part in them
That they find hard to tolerate at all

My dear caregivers
I really do thank you
For what you do for me

But won't you please try
To make a connection
Wouldn't we then both feel more human, more free?

An Abandoning Person

"Weak one,
I find you too much
I cannot reach out
Your heart to touch

For you trigger something deep inside
That I just cannot stand
The little person in me
That makes me feel less of a woman, less of a man

I want to engage
But deep down within
I can't get it right
I really can't win

Try to forgive
I know that you can
I've tried my best
Try to understand

But go I must
And go I will
I know you need me
I have to go still."

Lukewarm

Wear it 'round your neck
For everyone to see
Wear it on your arm
With your heart on your sleeve?

Or keep your feelings in tight
Never digging deep to say
That pain that you keep hidden
Find it hard to articulate?

"Come to me but go away
In my heart you cannot stay
Have no room for you
For my hurts I cherish I do

I cling to my hurts
They serve me well
The definition of strong
Is not to talk or to tell"

But I say to you that
Into the hands of God
Is where these hurts really belong

To bring them forward
And to face them
Is what truly makes you strong

That would give God

A chance to make it right
You could give Him your hurts
Instead of holding them tight

"I just though seem to sit
On a fence between hot and cold
Can't take that step of faith
Days pass and I grow old

Lukewarm* I guess I am
I guess I do need to grow
Beyond this fence
I see now I need to go."

*Revelation 3:16 (Jesus' words): "So, because you are lukewarm—neither hot nor cold—I am about to spit you out of my mouth."

Ode to the Nurses

Such difficult work
Is what you do
Cleaning up messes
That we leave for you

You persevere
Even despite
Difficult patients
That test your might

Some of us do
Test you it's true
For we have so many needs

But thanks I do say
And applaud you today
For I couldn't do without you, indeed.

Six Arms and As Many Legs: Ode to the Nurses

"Six arms and as many legs
Is what I feel I need
To accomplish the task
That God sets before me

I have a good day
When most things go okay
But there are days when
So much goes wrong and then

Then I want to scream
Or maybe have a good cry
Stocks are low or out
And the in-charge makes me sigh

At home too I have
Troubles that are real
Hard not to bring
Them to work I feel

In many directions
I'm being pulled
Sometimes, for true

God help me
Keep it together
To serve people, to serve You."

Sour

I look at one nurse's face
And all I see is sour
I hear your voice
And inside I can cower

For your anger you use
As a weapon, as a tool
To keep me quiet
Make me your fool

But deep down inside
I remember a mum
Who filled with anger
Would make me dumb

Quiet and silent
Unable to assert
Myself, my responses
Would tend to be curt

For inside I recoiled in fear
From her anger and rage
My stomach all in a knot
Me unable to turn the page

Because as a child, I felt
So stuck in the pain
Not able to rise above
And see Son once again

And now I'm prone
To be triggered by
An angry nurse
And in pain I lie

Lie there for a bit
But I don't get stuck as much
Because indeed it is a sad person
Who belittles the vulnerable and such

Jesus helps me now to see
That she was mislead
Rage and hurt she herself
As a young one was likely fed

So I can forgive
And reach down a hand
As God has done to me
To help her to stand.

Contagious

Contagious
It's outrageous
But oh so true

Evil and goodness
All of it no less
Has a ripple effect from me to you

For good promotes good
When you witness true love
You'll want to know
What those folk are made of

With evil
Well, it's the same
With evil
It's no game

A complaining spirit
Is like a damp cloth
That spreads all around

Gossip can lead to more
And before you know it
Someone is literally torn down

With suicide, there's a ripple effect
If a crack in the foundation you do detect
It can lead to all crumbling down
Result in rubble right to the ground

Remember that suicide does leave
A trail of folk who grieve
And it really could inspire
Another to suicide, to conspire

I know you may be
In unrelenting pain
Know we are blessed though
By your movement forward again

So what I am saying is this
Remember that in what you do
People are watching and waiting
They might follow your example good or bad too.

Part 3: On Hope in Jesus

Turn and Trust

Turn and trust
The Savior true
For He really wants
You, yes you

You need to acknowledge
This problem called sin
You need to say yes
And let Jesus in

For He paid the price
He paid it in full
The penalty for your sin and mine

And He does forgive
No matter what
Time after time after time

Just say, "Jesus come in
Be the Lord of my soul
Forgive my sins, please make
Serving you my true goal"

For being holy

He cannot abide
By the sin in your heart
That you try to hide

So give it to Him
Give him your life, too
'Cause He freely gave His
For me and for you

Do it now, my friend
You know you really must
To be right with a holy God
You need to but turn and trust.

Deep, Deep Love

I get really scared sometimes
And I wonder whether
I can make this paraplegia fly

I wonder whether
I'll find and keep hope*
I wonder if I could go that high

And I wonder if I will find
True love again in my life
One who could embrace
Me and my disability strife

But in the meantime
I will go and build
On the friendships I have
And from You be filled

For I know that You love me
Through many and much
My family, my friends
Circumstances and such

You melt away the fear
And make me bold again
As I feel deep, deep love
From You, Jesus my friend.

*Five years post-injury, I am preaching, I am leading and co-ordinating an Adult Sunday School class, leading group therapy, and co-facilitating a depression/manic-depression support group, having helped lead about 38 people to faith in Christ.

Flowers in the Desert

I have a little cactus
All prickly and tough
Bristles and leather skin
That's what it's made of

On its surface

Grow star-shaped thorns
All symmetrical, each one
Growing from a single skin horn

But it's exterior betrays it
For from deep down within
Spring nine pink blossoms
From deep beneath the prickly skin

Nine radiant blossoms
In all pink, yellow and white
It really is
Quite a delightful sight*

I am a little cactus
All prickly and tough
But from deep down within
Surprisingly grow prettiness and beauty and such

Such like I've never known
Or could never believe to be
Out of a barren desert
A spiritual loveliness grows in me

So if you're dry
Just know
That spiritual
Flowers can grow

Where and when
You least expect
The creator of Whom

May be God I suspect.**

*This was an actual plant that I bought at a small store near the institution.

**This was written about eleven months after my injury when I had some doubt about the very existence of a loving God.

When I felt Jesus lift a great heavy burden off of me on a new level, the burden of the scapegoating I endured as a child, I wrote a trilogy of poems about freedom. Here they are:

Sweet Freeing Jesus

Sweet freeing Jesus
You make my heart sing
Close to your breast
Forever will I cling

I am so glad
To be able to say
That I love you more dearly
Than ever today

For you free me from chains
And fetters so strong
You knew it was wrong
To live with them on

You helped me shout, "Freedom!"
And throw them aside
Near by your side
You ask me to abide

For relentless is evil
So relentless I'll be
To find hope, to find love
To know what it is to be free

Thank you, dear Savior
For helping me see
That I was meant for You
And You were meant for me.

Flying with Jesus

Flying I do
I float like a bird
Soaring high above
Singing songs yet unheard

Flying I feel free
And truly happy
Didn't know, wouldn't believe
That such freedom I could receive

You heal me you do
I know that it's true

And I'll never be the same

Thank you for mending
Thank you for sending
Jesus—truly the name above any other name.

Jesus Frees Us

Jesus frees us
Sends us soaring
To heights and special places

He kindles and rekindles
The fire within and
Brings us into wide open spaces

Where He can show us
The truth of who we are
As individuals, as Christians
He brings near what was far

Far out of reach
Or so I thought
To search in and up
Is what He's taught

I really cannot say
Nor adequately put into words
All that I feel

All that I've heard

Heard from Jesus
As He teaches me His way
With Him forever
I believe I will stay.

What's Harder?

It's a shock
To go from walking to this
From walking each day
To true and permanent paralysis

"Forgive them, Father,
For they know not what they do"*
It is Jesus' call to me
It is Jesus' call to you

Not only for those who contributed
But for myself, I need
To be able to deeply forgive**

For this is
The key to
Truly and freely live

What's harder, I'm sure
I really don't know

Paralysis or forgiveness
Do teach me, please show

That I can learn both
And freedom to find
A freedom actually of
The spiritual kind.

*Luke 23:34 (Jesus' words while on the cross): "Father, forgive them, for they do not know what they are doing."
**Matthew 6:14-15 (Jesus' words): "For if you forgive men when they sin against you, your heavenly Father will also forgive you. But if you do not forgive men their sins, your Father will not forgive your sins."

Routine

I live in a world of routine
Where regimentation rules
But that, in fact, can be seen
As the very tool

That God uses to produce
Endurance of spirit and faith
Endurance of heart
A toughness it makes

Resiliency of spirit

Not hardness though
You can be a conduit
As you let His love flow

You need to know
And be able to discern
What to take, when to say no
You really need to learn

To let in and let out
Just like a breath
Take in the good
And discard the rest

Routine's a constant flow
That's how we become
A diamond—it's coal under pressure

A flower will wilt
And eventually give way
To fruit, then seed that is hidden treasure

And from a single seed
Many more can come
So let go and let God work
Right 'til He's done

For it is through
Structure and routine
That perseverance, character
And hope* can be seen.

*Romans 5:3:   "(W)e also rejoice in our sufferings, because we know that suffering produces perseverance; perseverance, character; and character, hope."

A Gentleman

He is a gentleman
He doesn't take over and step in
He asks us merely to come
Come and follow Him

He gently leads
So quietly and softly too
He does it so tenderly
Look! He even calls you!

He will not force
Himself upon anyone
But He doesn't stop calling
'Til your life is done

For suffering and death
Are yet but tools
He uses to draw you near

To break down anger
To fill you with wonder
To help you face your deepest fear
Deep suffering

A precious gift
With it He does
Want to lift

Lift you up
To higher ground
With Him is where you belong

That's why it urges
In Scripture time and again
Be courageous and be strong*

For Jesus is a gentleman
He only whispers to you
He asks you to listen
And then obey Him too

You can choose
To go your own sweet way
But you reap what you sow**
Both now and on Judgment Day.***

*Deuteronomy 31:6,7,23; Joshua 1:7,9,18; 10:25;
1 Chronicles 22:13,20; 28:20; 2 Chronicles 32:7
**Galatians 6:7: "A man reaps what he sows";
2 Corinthians 9:6: "Remember this: Whoever sows
sparingly will also reap sparingly, and whoever sows generously will also reap generously."
***Ecclesiastes 12:14: "For God will bring every deed
into judgment, including every hidden thing, whether it
is good or evil"; Hebrews 9:27a: "(M)an is destined to
die once, and after that to face judgment."

Substitute Saviors

"You've got to go to the lonesome valley,
No one can go there for you

You've got to go to the lonesome valley,
No one can go there for you"*

What do you lean on
Would it be sex,
Would it be a john?

Booze, other people, your own will
Do you rely at your core
On these things still?

What do you clutch
What is your crutch
To help you get by
Do you live in a lie?

Hatred, bitterness, rage
These can take us away
Hanging on to these
Crippled we will stay

Substitute saviours
Don't properly fill the hole
It's only through Jesus
That we become spiritually whole

For salvation, our best is yet unacceptable
We need to get forgiveness for sin
He needs to heal the state,
The condition we find ourselves in

Then, counseling, for deep healing
He may guide you to
As you work through tough emotions
And find His courage within you

For "you've got to go to the lonesome valley
No one can go there for you

You've got to go to the lonesome valley
No one can go there for you."*

*Taken from a song entitled, "Lonesome
Valley" by Fairfield Four of the *O Brother,
Where Art Thou?* soundtrack

Breath

I have breath
I have been given breath
I can breathe
And feel free
To be just what I am

Lost at times

Sinner always
I am free to be me
Just me
Simple and true
I'm not anyone else
I'm not you

But you as well can be
Free and hopeful too
You can find peace
In what you are and do

I pray His peace
Upon your ways
With Him abide
And with you He stays*

Look in and up
And you will find
Hope everlasting
In body, soul and mind

Trust me today
'Cause I think I've found the way
To make life so worthwhile

I really do believe
If Him you receive
He will turn your frown to a smile.**

*John 15:4a (Jesus' words): "Remain in me, and I will
remain in you."

**Isaiah 61:3: "He (The Lord) has sent me (the prophet) to bestow on them … the oil of gladness instead of mourning."

My Only Hope

They went from in my head
To in reality instead
Can't get away
From voices even today

For I have to hear
The words of those near
Secondhand conversations I do
Have to listen to

The nurses in the hall
Make such a racket for true
That I cannot find some
Quiet space for me or for you

A quiet little space
Is all I want to find
On God's green earth
Away from the daily grind…

…of the institution
No one can flourish here
I find I need something

Maybe rye, maybe beer

What I have is Someone
Jesus Christ, my Savior
To Him I'll cling
And pray all the more

Because He is Strength
And He is Hope
With Him alone
Is how I'll cope

Sometimes it seems
That He doesn't do that much
Doesn't take away
The pain or the suffering as such

But with it He molds
He strengthens He does
So go on dear Jesus, just help me

To seek You
All the time
For my only hope rests in thee.

I Folded My Hands

I folded my hands to pray
I was in a prison
I reached to the Son
Who died and had risen

I asked him
His strength to give
To endure the bars
To help me live

The prison bars faded
In the light of Him
As the world around me
Grew strangely dim

All I could see
While being in the Light
Was Him and Him alone
It almost filled me with fright

For He is so real
Or has made Himself to be
Inside He is my Hope
Stay, dear Lord, always near to me.

Approaching Spring

The thaw is on, in more ways than one
On our streets as well as in our hearts
Trickle of activity as folk start
To shake off the winter blahs

Heavy coats are shed
Mittens and hats too
There is an aliveness in the air
For me and for you

Birds are singing and seem
To be flying more free
As the great weight of winter
Comes off them and me

For the world is awakening
From a slumber, a cold
It's putting on the new
And shedding the old

Trees are coming to bud
And the sun again feels warm
Replacing with a lightness
The deep, dark snow storm

That was so ominous
Just a few short weeks ago
Now there are everywhere
Rivers of melting snow

I never did appreciate
Or feel quite so strong
The newness of the day
As it gets progressively long

For You mold something
Through the winter of our souls
That brings life and freedom anew

Please help me, Jesus
Understand Your ways
Or at least in all, see You.

Inaccessibility

Buildings I see
Inaccessibility
Stairs and more stairs
Adding to my cares

I approach my friend
And she does let me in
No steps to contend with
Smooth sailing with Him

For Jesus can help us overcome*
The barriers to our hearts
He's freely loving
Right from the start

And He helps us to be
In His love and feel free
Free to reach and take a stand
For justice for every woman, child and man

Yet His eternal nature is not
Totally accessible to the finite mind
For His ways, His thoughts
Are of a unique, one-of-a-kind**

But ask your questions
Your why ones too
In Him are still the answers
For both me and for you

And when you don't find answers
To all God says and does
Know that faith is the bridge
And in mystery still lies love.

*John 16:33 (Jesus' words): "In this world you will have trouble. But take heart! I have overcome the world."
**Isaiah 55:8: "'For my thoughts are not your thoughts, neither are your ways my ways,' declares the Lord."

Secret Sin

Secret sin
Is there such a thing?

What do you do
Pornography, lust too?
What is needed is that
You get clean through and through

You need to go to Him
In repentance and holy fear*
He's the one to heal
He'll wipe every tear**

For He knows
Maybe you and He alone
To Him your sin
Is thoroughly known

It's your relationship
To Him that matters truly
You need to get right with Him
Then you can come to me

Confess your sins
One to another***
Seek God first
Then go to your brother

Whatever it is

It grieves Him so
Won't you into His hands
I urge you, let it go?

*Psalm 111:10a: "The fear of the Lord is the beginning of wisdom."
**Isaiah 25:8: "The Sovereign Lord will wipe away the tears from all faces;" Revelation 7:17c: "And God will wipe away every tear from their eyes."
***James 5:16: "Therefore confess your sins to each other and pray for each other so that you may be healed."

A Little Plant

A little plant
All droopy and dry
Needs to be watered
Please do, please try

If you water it a lot
And do it all in one shot
It cannot absorb it for true

It needs a little bit
You need to water it
Many times, and often too

For the water is held
Better as time goes by

As you give little by little
Time after time after time

So please if you can
Throw it a line
Maybe you think little difference it'll make

But I assure you
Even this cactus
Grows with the little at a time I take.

Confined

Confined
In my body
And in my mind

For I want to fly
But for real, can I
With a heart full of fear?

It holds me back
And keeps me in black
As I shed tear upon tear

For I cannot overcome
This trial on my own
So give it to You, I will, Lord
For your faithfulness* You've shown…

...to me time and again
Certainly, it's in the Book
Help me to really focus
And have a good look

At your doing right
Helping sufferers pull through
Good is where You want me
Good You'll lead me to**

Maybe not
Of the physical kind
You might not take the suffering away

But You will sow
Treasures in my spirit
If, with You, I will stay***

So, no matter how it looks
To the finite mind
Help me to rest in faith
When answers I cannot find

Lord, let us all break out
Of spiritual confinement
Make us who You want
Lord, do Your refinement.

*Psalm 85:9-10: "Surely his salvation is near those who fear him, that his glory may dwell in our land. Love and faithfulness meet together; righteousness and peace kiss each other."

**Psalm 85:12: "The Lord will indeed give what is good;"
Romans 8:28: "And we know that in all things God works
for the good of those who love him, who have been called
according to his purpose."
***John 15:5 (Jesus' words): "I am the vine; you are the
branches. If a man remains in me and I in him, he will
bear much fruit; apart from me you can do nothing."

See Me Through

We turn away and sin
Deny Him access in
And His heart does feel the pain

Of separation
From the destination
To be like Jesus through the rain

The sting of sin
Produces a gap
Between me and a loving Savior

But as I repent
And plead for
His mercy all the more…

…He doesn't even blink
But accepts me right back
Forgiving as He goes

He's not like us
For we hold on
To anger and to our woes

What an awesome privilege
To call Jesus my friend
Please stay with me and see me through
Right to the very end.

Little Birds

Little birds
I see you fly
I used to be envious of this

I see you now
Land and hop
You're doing what I miss

I really am angry
My blood does boil
At Your allowing this
And bringing such toil

For I do not understand
Nor yet do I see
Why You have allowed
Such profound misery

To befall a little person
To befall a little girl
Though I know You can create
From a common grain of sand, a pearl

So weave your web
Lord, do your work
I'll stay right close to you

For I know
In You are
Still the answers for true.

The following poem was written on the first day that I was allowed out of the building at the institution as we had been restricted to it for four weeks due to the SARS scare in March of 2003. I went to sit in the garden and wrote this poem:

Freedom

When we think of freedom
We think of things like this
Walking on an open beach
Lovemaking sealed with a kiss

We think of horseback rides

Playground slides
Cars and bicycles too

We don't think of wheelchairs
And their enemies, the stairs
As being instruments of truth*

But there is a freedom
Of a spiritual kind
That brings hope and love anew

It grows in our hearts
In the midst of
The profound suffering we do

So please embrace
Your suffering for true
Jesus is trying to make
You more like Him, yes you.

*John 8:31-32: "To the Jews who had believed him, Jesus said, 'If you hold to my teaching you are really my disciples. Then you will know the truth, and the truth will set you free.'"

A Pearl

Though you feel heavy
And burdened with care

And it's a long road
From here to there

Here in the intensity
Of the grief you feel
It's hard to believe you can
Be content* again for real

But, "my yoke is easy
And my burden is light"**
He is the Master
At making us bright

Bright stars for Him
It's always what He hopes
That you will take your trials
And do more than just cope

Rejoice in suffering***
It seems absurd
Seems like the craziest
Thing I've ever heard

But rejoice we can
And rejoice we will
If, through our trials
We cleave to Him still

For it is hard
To love the very One
Who allowed the great sorrow
When all is said and done

But if we bring it to Jesus
We can watch as He makes
A pearl from the common grain
Of sand that He takes.

*Philippians 4:11b-13 (Paul in prison):

"I have learned to be content whatever the
circumstances. I know what it is to be in
need and I know what it is to have plenty. I
have learned the secret of being content in
any and every situation, whether well fed or
hungry, whether living in plenty or in want. I
can do everything through him who gives me
strength."

**Matthew 11:28-30 (Jesus' words): "Come to me, all
you who are weary and burdened, and I will give you
rest. Take my yoke upon you and learn from me, for I am
gentle and humble in heart, and you will find rest for your
souls. For my yoke is easy and my burden is light."
***Romans 5:2b-4: "And we rejoice in the hope of the
glory of God. Not only so but we also rejoice in our
sufferings, because we know that suffering produces perseverance; perseverance, character; and character, hope;"
1 Peter 4:13: "But rejoice that you participate in the sufferings of Christ, so that you may be overjoyed when his
glory is revealed."

Death Dew

Everyday
So hard
To push it away

Death dew
Collects
Each day anew

A fresh layer descends
On me this very day
Can't help but wish
That it would just have its way

Ready to go and find relief
From the endless barrage of pain
Cried so many tears of grief
Again and again and again

Tired of the struggle
And of the fight too
Rather wish sweet death
Would embrace me, would do

Do its work
For I've made my peace
With my Savior, Jesus
Now I seek relief

But You want to bring

Glory through the pain*
Draw others, and me to You

As others reach out to me
They find they are
Discovering You, for true**

So please help me, Lord
Temptations to suicide to shun
For I will wait for Your time
Not my will, but Yours be done.***

*Hebrews 2:10: "In bringing many sons to glory, it was fitting that God, for whom and through whom everything exists, should make the author of their salvation perfect through suffering;" Philippians 3:10–11 (my prayer as well): "I want to know Christ and the power of his resurrection and the fellowship of sharing in his sufferings, becoming like him in his death, and so somehow, to attain to the resurrection from the dead;" 1 Peter 4:12–13: "Dear friends, do not be surprised at the painful trial you are suffering, as though something strange were happening to you. But rejoice that you participate in the sufferings of Christ, so that you may be overjoyed when his glory is revealed."

**Matthew 25:40 (Jesus' words): "I tell you the truth, whatever you did for one of the least of these brothers of mine, you did for me."

***Matthew 26:39 finds Jesus in His Garden of Gethsemane, saying, "My Father, if it is possible, may this cup be taken from me. Yet not as I will, but as you will."

Psalm 48:14: "For this God is our God for ever and ever; he will be our guide even to the end."

Endnotes

Introduction

1 Revelation 21:4
2 Genesis 3:17b
3 John16:33
4 John14:6
5 Matthew 11:28-30
6 Hebrews 9:27
7 John 1:3
8 Philippians 1:20
9 1 Corinthians 6:19-20
10 Isaiah 46:4
11 Romans 8:17
12 Philippians 3:10-11

Chapter 1: Patience

1 1 Corinthians 13:4
2 Ephesians 5:15-16
3 Ephesians 6:10-12
4 Philippians 1:6
5 Matthew 19:19, 22:39;
  Mark 12:31,33;
  Luke 10:27;
  Romans 13:9;
  Galatians 5:14;
  James 2:8
6 Romans 8:1
7 Proverbs 11:14
8 Luke 23:34

9 Luke 15:20
10 Psalm 103:11-12
11 Matthew 6:14-15
12 2 Corinthians 5:17
13 Matthew 11:28-30
14 Isaiah 61:3
15 1 John 1:9
16 Matthew 9:10-13
17 Titus 3:3-5
18 Matthew 5:7
19 Luke 6:36
20 Matthew 16:8
   Luke 12:28
21 Mark 16:14
22 Matthew 9:13
23 Habakkuk 3:2b
24 Matthew 5:7
25 Jeremiah 29:11
26 Genesis 1:31
27 John 10:11
28 1 Peter 4:13

Chapter 2: On Accepting – Part 1

1   John 8:32
2   Ephesians 6:12
3   Genesis 3:17b
4   Matthew 6:34
5   Deuteronomy 31:6, 8;
    Joshua 1:5;
    Hebrews 13:5
6   Psalm 23:4

8   2 Corinthians 12:9a
9   2 Corinthians 12:9b-10
10 Philippians 4:12b-13
11 2 Corinthians 11:30
12 2 Corinthians 10b
13 Nehemiah 8:10
14 2 Corinthians 3:18

Chapter 6: I am Richer

1   Philippians 3:7-11
2   John 10:28
3   Romans 8:38-39
4   Deuteronomy 5:17
    Exodus 20:13
5   Hebrews 4:14-15
6   2 Thessalonians 3:5
7   Genesis 1:31
8   Psalm 139:14
9   1 Corinthians 6:19-20
10 Deuteronomy 5:26;
    Exodus 20:12

Chapter 7: I Fought Suicide

1   p. 611. Concise Oxford Dictionary of Current
        English .R.E. Allen, editor. Clarendon Press,
        Oxford. 1991.
2   Jeremiah 29:11
3   Deuteronomy 31:6, ;
    Joshua 1:5
4   2 Timothy 1:8-9

5 Jeremiah 29:11

Chapter 8: In the Case of Mental Illness

1 Ephesians 6:12

Chapter 9: The Nature of "Suicidality" in Mental Illness

1 John 13:34-35
2 1 Corinthians 13:4a, 5b
3 Job 1:20b-22
4 Job 2:5
5 Job 2:5
6 Job 2:9
7 Job 2:10
8 Job 2:10
9 Job 2:10
10 Isaiah 40:29-31
11 Romans 5:2b-5
12 Romans 5:8
13 Galatians 5:22-23
14 John 15:1-2

Chapter 10: The Power of Prayer

1 Matthew 7:7
2 Matthew 26:40-41
3 James 1:13
4 Matthew 26:38
5 Matthew 26:38b
6 Matthew 26:39b

7   Matthew 26:42b
8   Matthew 26:38
9   Matthew 26:39

Chapter 11: "Going On is Tougher"

1   Isaiah 61:3
2   Mark 12:29
3   Matthew 22:38
4   Mark 12:29-30
5   Matthew 22:39;
    Mark 12:31
6   John 3:3
7   John 14:6
8   Luke 15:10
9   Ephesians 2:8-9
10 Nehemiah 8:10b
11 Ephesians 6:12
12 Ephesians 6:13
13 Proverbs 6:10-11, 24:33-34
14 1 John 4:4b
15 Philippians 1:6
16 Matthew 11:28-30
17 Ecclesiastes 3:1

Chapter 12: Some Relevant Scripture

1   Luke 18:1
2   Luke 18:4b-8a
3   Matthew 26:41
4   John 16:33

Chapter 13: More Relevant Scripture

1   1 Samuel 17:47
2   2 Chronicles 20:15
3   Exodus 14:14
4   2 Corinthians 1:6;
     Revelation 1:9, 13:10, 14:12
5   2 Timothy 3:16
6   Matthew 4:5-7
7   Philippians 4:13
8   Matthew 24:36, 42
9   Titus 2:11-14
10 John 10:25
11 Matthew 11:5-6

Chapter 14: Self Esteem

1   Romans 8:28

Chapter 15: Suicidal Predisposition – Part 2

1   Mark 12:28-31
2   Matthew 26:36-46
3   Proverbs 4:23

Chapter 16: "My Brother's Keeper"

1   Genesis 4:9
2   John 13:35
3   Matthew 25:40
4   Ezekiel 21:26a, 27a
5   Isaiah 55:8

Chapter 17: Suffering Quietly

1   Matthew 5:44
2   Galatians 5:23
3   Mark 10:21
4   1 Corinthians 9:22a
5   John 8:32

Chapter 18: "Pleasure" in Illness

1   Matthew 19:26
2   Matthew 16:24;
    Mark 8:34
3   Matthew 26:39
4   Luke 9:23
5   Matthew 6:34
6   2 Corinthians 11:30
7   2 Corinthians 12:7
8   2 Corinthians 12:9
9   Philippians 1:6
10 Philippians 1:21-26
11 Matthew 6:19-21
12 Ephesians 6:8

Chapter 20: Disabled

1   1 Corinthians 7:8-9
2   Colossians 3:5
3   Galatians 5:16-17
4   Romans 7:15-19
5   John 8:7, 9

6 John 8:11
7 Galatians 5:22-23
8 Hebrews 11:25-26

Chapter 21: Ellen's Recipe for Life

1 Psalm 1:1-2, 111:2; Joshua 1:8; Luke 2:19
2 Matthew 26:39
3 John 10:10
4 James 1:14
5 Jeremiah 17:9
6 Isaiah 61:3
7 Isaiah 55:8
8 Job 42:3b, 4b
9 Matthew 22:37-38

Chapter 22: Relentless Agony—Grief Expressed

1 2 Corinthians 1:3-4

Chapter 23: The Vulnerable

1 Matthew 25:40
2 Genesis 4:9
3 Matthew 23:12

Chapter 24: On Scripture

1 Ephesians 3:18-19
2 John 13:34
3 Isaiah 55:8
4 Matthew 22:38

5   John 1:3
6   Romans 8:39
7   Matthew 6:20
8   1 Corinthians 6:19-20
9   Psalm 139:14
10 John 10:10
11 Colossians 1:16b-17
12 Numbers 11:15
13 Jonah 4:3
14 1 Kings 19:4
15 1 Kings 19:9a
16 Job 3:1-10
17 Job 4:7, 8:20, 11:13-15
18 Job 38:3
19 Job 38:4-5a
20 Job 42:10
21 Job 42:12
22 John 16:33
23 1 Peter 4:12-13
24 Isaiah 53:3a

Chapter 25: A Dynamic Relationship

1   John 1:3
2   Genesis 2:7, 22
3   Genesis 1:31
4   1 Corinthians 6:19-20
5   Luke 15:11-32
6   Jeremiah 29:11
7   Philippians 1:6
8   Mark 4:35-41
9   Colossians 1:16b

10 Isaiah 55:8
11 Ezekiel 21:27
12 1 Thessalonians 5:3
13 2 Thessalonians 1:9
14 Proverbs 3:12;
     Hebrews 12:6
15 Ephesians 3:20-21

Chapter 26: On Free Will

1 Isaiah 55:8
2 Ephesians 6:12-13
3 Job 3:1-10
4 Job 3:11
5 Job 42:12-17
6 Malachi 3:2
7 Psalm 139:14
8 Philippians 3:13b-14

Chapter 27: Physical Comfort and Happiness

1 Philippians 3:7-8a
2 John 12:31
3 Matthew 6:20
4 John 14:6
5 John 3:3

Chapter 28: There Can Come a Point

1 Isaiah 55:8
2 Psalm 139:13-14a

3   2 Thessalonians 3:5
4   Matthew 11:30
5   Genesis 1:31

Chapter 28: More on Job

1   Job 3:3
2   Job 3:11
3   Job 3:16
4   Job 40:4
5   Job 42:2-3, 5-6
6   Job 42:10
7   Philippians 4:12b-13
8   1 Corinthians 13:4-8a

Chapter 30: Trying Too Hard

1   Isaiah 55:8

Chapter 31: Intrusiveness

1   1 Corinthians 13:4
2   John 8:32
3   Matthew 11:28-30

Chapter 32: On Prayer

1   Job 6:14
2   2 Corinthians 1:8
3   2 Corinthians 1:10-11a
4   Colossians 3:1-2
5   Isaiah 55:8

6   2 Corinthians 12:9
7   Exodus 20:3;
    Deuteronomy 5:7

Chapter 33: Every Little Bit Counts

1   Philippians 4:8;
    Colossians 3:2
2   1 Thessalonians 5:18
3   Matthew 25:40
4   Psalm 77:2b
5   Psalm 77:4b
6   Psalm 77:7
7   Psalm 77:8
8   Psalm 77:8
9   Psalm 77:9
10 Psalm 77:11
11 Philippians 1:6
12 Acts 24:15;
    Romans 6:5

Chapter 34: Saying "No"

1   Matthew 19:19, 22:39;
    Mark 12:31, 33;
    Luke 10:27;
    Romans 13:9;
    Galatians 5:14;
    James 2:8
2   Matthew 8:20
3   John 14:1-3
4   John 12:31

5 Romans 12:15
6 Matthew 12:36;
  Romans 14:12;
  Hebrews 4:13
7 Revelation 21:4
8 Matthew 22:38
9 Matthew 22:37
10 Matthew 22:39